FREE DVD   **FREE DVD**

Miller Analogies Test (MAT) DVD from Trivium Test Prep!

Dear Customer,

Thank you for purchasing from Trivium Test Prep! We're honored to help you prepare for your exam.

To show our appreciation, we're offering a **FREE *MFT Essential Test Tips* DVD by Trivium Test Prep**. Our DVD includes 35 test preparation strategies that will make you successful on your exam. All we ask is that you email us your feedback and describe your experience with our product. Amazing, awful, or just so-so: we want to hear what you have to say!

To receive your **FREE *MFT Essential Test Tips* DVD**, please email us at 5star@triviumtestprep.com. Include "Free 5 Star" in the subject line and the following information in your email:

1. The title of the product you purchased.
2. Your rating from 1 – 5 (with 5 being the best).
3. Your feedback about the product, including how our materials helped you meet your goals and ways in which we can improve our products.
4. Your full name and shipping address so we can send your **FREE *MFT Essential Test Tips* DVD**.

If you have any questions or concerns please feel free to contact us directly at 5star@triviumtestprep.com. Thank you!

- **Trivium Test Prep Team**

Copyright © 2019 by Trivium Test Prep

ALL RIGHTS RESERVED. By purchase of this book, you have been licensed one copy for personal use only. No part of this work may be reproduced, redistributed, or used in any form or by any means without prior written permission of the publisher and copyright owner. Trivium Test Prep; Cirrus Test Prep; Accepted, Inc.; and Ascencia Test Prep are all imprints of Trivium Test Prep, LLC.

AMFTRB was not involved in the creation or production of this product, is not in any way affiliated with Trivium Test Prep, and does not sponsor or endorse this product. All test names (and their acronyms) are trademarks of their respective owners. This study guide is for general information and does not claim endorsement by any third party.

Table of Contents

Introduction 5

Chapter 1: MFT Models 7

Chapter 2: The Practice of MFT 53

Chapter 3: Professional Ethics 65

Test Your Knowledge 79

Test Your Knowledge—Answers 97

Additional Study Resources.. 99

Introduction

The Association of Marital and Family Therapy Regulatory Board (AMFTRB) created and standardized the national Marriage and Family Therapy (MFT) exam. Most states use the standard exam provided by the AMFTRB as a part of their required criteria for issuing a state license to practice marital and family therapy.* Examinees are expected to demonstrate what has been deemed by test administrators as the minimum knowledge necessary to practice family and marital therapy. This includes knowledge of the major therapy models used in the MFT field, issues relevant to conducting treatment (e.g., assessment, treatment design), and ethical guidelines used by professionals in the field. Currently, the exam is composed of 200 multiple choice questions.

In order to sit for the national MFT exam, held during certain intervals each year, one must first apply to take the exam and be approved by his/her state board to do so. Generally, approval is based on academic credentials (e.g., the completion of an approved graduate or post-graduate degree program in family and marital therapy) and experiential credentials (e.g., the completion of a specific number of supervised clinical training hours providing relational therapy). Specific application requirements to sit for the exam vary from state to state.

For more information on exam administration (e.g., state boards, applications, cost, exam dates) and exam construction (e.g., test domains, content), please refer to the AMFTRB's web site: www.amftrb.org.

* **Note:** This guide is intended for use to prepare for the national MFT exam in most U.S. states. However, the state of California does not currently use the AMFTRB's standard exam. California residents wishing to take the MFT exam should refer to the California Board of Consumer Sciences website for state exam information: www.bbs.ca.gov.

Chapter 1: MFT Models

The national MFT exam in large part is designed to assess test-takers' knowledge of major models of marital and family therapy and the way they used to design and conduct treatment at various stages including assessment, diagnosis, intervention, evaluation, and termination. The following provides an overview of the models that are typically included on the exam. For each model listed here, the following is provided: overview, leading figures, key concepts, and therapy (goals, assessment, and interventions/techniques).

Attachment Theory

Overview

According to Attachment Theory, all human beings need emotional and psychological attachment to others in order to survive and thrive. The need for this attachment begins immediately at birth, and infants have attachment needs that are ideally satisfied by a parent, namely, the mother. Depending on the attachment style that one develops with his/her mother, relationship dynamics formed later in life will be influenced and will result in various adult "attachment styles."

Some of the central tenets of attachment theory include the following:

- ❖ A primary motivation for people is the process of seeking and maintaining contact with others. An innate characteristic of being human is dependency.

- ❖ Contact and connection with others is an innate survival mechanism. The presence of an attachment figure provides comfort and security, while the absence of this creates psychological distress and in some cases, disorder. Positive attachments create a "secure base" from which individuals can operate and most readily respond and adapt to their environment. Positive attachments also create a psychological "safe haven" and thus buffers the effect of stress and an optimal development environment.

- ❖ Responsiveness and emotional accessibility are the building blocks of secure bonds. This is the same for adult-adult relationships (e.g., couples) and child-parent relationships.

- ❖ Attachment behaviors are triggered, when a bond's security is threatened. If these behaviors fail to evoke responsiveness from the attachment figure, a negative process occurs, which may involve anger, protest, clinging, despair, or eventual detachment.

Leading Figures

- ❖ John Bowlby
- ❖ Mary Ainsworth

Key Concepts

Attachment style:

Adult style	Self is:	Others are:
Secure	Lovable	Reliable, responsive, able to be trusted
Anxious	Lovable?	Unreliable, maybe unresponsive
Avoidant Fearful	Not lovable	Unreliable, relationships to be feared
Avoidant Dismissing	Not lovable	Unreliable, others' attempts at relationships are not genuine

Attachment needs: common ones include the need to:

- ❖ Be and feel loved
- ❖ Be accepted
- ❖ Be comforted
- ❖ Be understood
- ❖ Be validated
- ❖ Receive empathy
- ❖ Trust that a partner/family member is going to be there in time of need and/or desperation

Therapy

Attachment Theory provides the theoretical basis for several family therapy models such as emotionally focused therapy and therapy based on Bowen

Family Systems Theory. Providing therapy based on this theory involves tasks such as providing a safe therapeutic environment, exploring current relationships, exploring the client-therapist relationship, and exploring how past relationships and experiences shape current relational patterns.

Attachment Theory is particularly useful for couples therapy. Couples therapy based on this theory (e.g., emotionally focused therapy) focuses on aspects like:

- ❖ Using emotion as the agent of therapeutic change
- ❖ The attachment needs of partners and systems of disengagement or engagement
- ❖ Creating a "safe space" for partners to be authentic within therapy sessions
- ❖ Shaping new bonding responses between partners
- ❖ Addressing "attachment injuries" or disruptions

The goal of couples therapy based on Attachment Theory is to address attachment concerns, reduce attachment insecurities, and create a secure bond between partners. Refer to the section "Emotionally Focused Therapy" for detailed information about this model of therapy.

Bowen Family Systems Theory

Overview

Bowen Family Systems Theory is a classic approach used in family therapy and is one of the most well known within the field. The theory was born out of Murray Bowen's clinical work as a psychiatrist and findings as a family researcher. It is an intergenerational theory, and a key tenet is that families pass on emotional and behavioral patterns across generations. As are many theories of family therapy, Bowen Family Systems Theory is rooted in Natural Systems Theory, viewing families as organisms capable of achieving growth and evolving as a unit and viewing individual members as interdependent on one another and capable of exerting great power over each other through emotional and behavioral processes.

It addresses relationships, regardless of whether or not the client is an individual, couple, or family. When Bowen Theory is used clinically with individuals, a client's family relationships are examined primarily from the individual point of view. However, techniques such as the "going home" task and process questions are used to involve other family members in the change process, even if only in a symbolic fashion.

Leading Figures

- ❖ Philip Guerin
- ❖ Michael Kerr
- ❖ Monica McGoldrick
- ❖ Betty Carter
- ❖ Murray Bowen

Key Concepts

The key concepts for treating families using the Bowen approach include:

- ❖ **Differentiation of self:** One's ability to distinguish and separate his/her own emotional and intellectual functioning from that of others, particularly family members, as well as one's ability to balance dependence and connectedness with others and personal autonomy. The degree to which a person's "self" is developed is considered one's level of differentiation. A person who is differentiated, according to Bowen, can respond to stresses with high levels of self-control and intellectual processing, minus excessive emotionality, which may contribute to irrational responses. A differentiated person can still respond to others with strong emotions and passion, but possesses the self-control that prevents impulsive behavior driven purely by emotional reactivity. Differentiated people are also able to take firm positions on issues that are presented to them. On the other hand, an undifferentiated individual often reacts to others around them with high levels of emotionality and low levels of self-control. Undifferentiated people tend to be emotionally fused and behave in a submissive manner in relation to others. Lack of autonomy also characterizes undifferentiated people. Emotions and cognitions may be blurred through the eyes of an undifferentiated person, as they generally have a harder time distinguishing what they think from what they feel.

- ❖ **Differentiation scale:** The level of differentiation of self is measured on a scale from 0 to 100. A person who falls toward the score of 0 on the differentiation of self scale has very low levels of differentiation or none at all. People toward 0 have very small solid selves and very large pseudo-selves. On the other end of the scale toward the score of 100 falls individuals with very small pseudo-selves and very large solid selves, and these people are highly or fully differentiated. Those on the lower end are thought to be more prone to chronic mental health issues. See below for an example of a differentiation scale.

Example Differentiation Scale

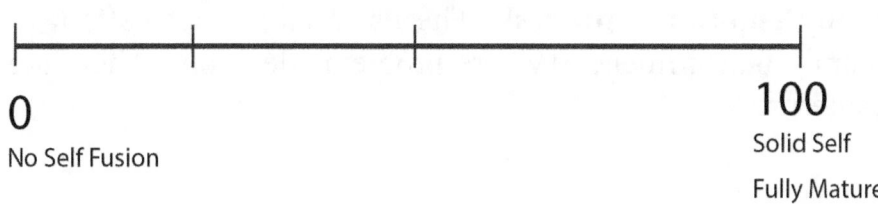

0
No Self Fusion

100
Solid Self
Fully Mature

- ❖ **Emotional cutoff:** Either discontinuing physical contact with others or maintaining contact, but avoiding discussion of emotional issues. This is done in an effort to manage unresolved problems and often to reduce one's own anxiety related to problems. Bowen contended that emotionally cutoff people are scared and threatened by intimacy and that the act of emotional cutoff is sometimes mistaken for maturity.

- ❖ **Family life cycle:** A concept refined by Betty Carter and Monica McGoldrick; it refers to the common stages by which families develop and change across the lifespan (e.g., "leaving home" stage during which young adults leave home; "joining of families through marriage" stage during which marriage occurs and a newly formed nuclear family system emerges).

- ❖ **Family projection process:** The psychological process through which parents' emotional issues are transferred to their children. For example, parents may give special attention to one child in the family out of fear that the child has the same mental health disorder that another family member has, regardless of whether or not the child has actually shown symptoms. This transmission can create psychological symptoms or disorder in children.

- **Fusion:** Emotional over-connectedness with another family member characteristic of undifferentiated people. Fusion results in not being able to make one's own decisions or form one's own opinions, but rather the echoing of those of the person with which one is fused.

- **Multigenerational transmission process:** The projection of the nuclear family emotional process onto successive generations within a family. This process often results in the transmission of chronic anxiety throughout generations of a family, particularly with children who are the most emotionally fused, or involved, with the family.

- **Nuclear family emotional process:** The basic emotional pattern or force in a family that influences where problems develop. There are four basic patterns:

    o Marital conflict
    o Dysfunction in a spouse
    o Impairment of a child or children
    o Emotional distance

    Related to this concept, **undifferentiated family ego mass** is an emotional force in which families are excessively emotionally reactive and possess low levels of differentiation, resulting in problems such as marital conflict.

- **Sibling position:** The position that children are born into in their families and which is thought to influence behaviors and emotions both within and outside of their families of origin. This concept cannot exactly predict the personality traits of children based on their sibling position, but offers a general way to view the roles that some children take on within their families of origin. For example, first-borns may have a tendency to use power and authority to exercise their dominance in their relations with others or be high achievers while laterborns may be more rebellious, challenge authority more, or be more open to new experiences than firstborns.

- **Societal emotional process:** The influence of the society in which a family exists has on them. Societies may influence families in a number of ways. For example, Bowen recognized that sexism, classism, and racism are all negative societal influences that affect families. Families and their individual members are better equipped to resist these negative influences with higher levels of differentiation.

- ❖ **Triangles:** A three-person relationship system, which often develops to deal with relationship tension that began between two people. Related to this, the unhealthy pattern of **triangulation** involves avoiding conflict between two people by bringing in a third person or entity (e.g., work) to decrease tension, reduce anxiety, and help stabilize the relationship between the two people. According to Bowen's theory, once a third party plays a regular, integral role within the relationship of the original two people, a triangle becomes fixed.

Therapy

Bowenian therapy's aim is to improve individual and family functioning and shift dysfunctional patterns into healthier ones by increasing awareness and understanding and decreasing emotional reactivity. A major tool used during assessment is the **genogram**, which is a family diagram similar to a family tree, but includes emotional processes in addition to facts and names (see example below). The most common techniques used in Bowenian therapy include the use of genograms (as both an assessment and intervention tool), family interviews with **process questions** (questions designed to explore emotional patterns), and the **"going home" task** (involves having clients visit their families of origin with goals such as gathering new information about family patterns, reconnecting with cutoff members, and interacting with members in new ways).

Example genogram and common genogram symbols

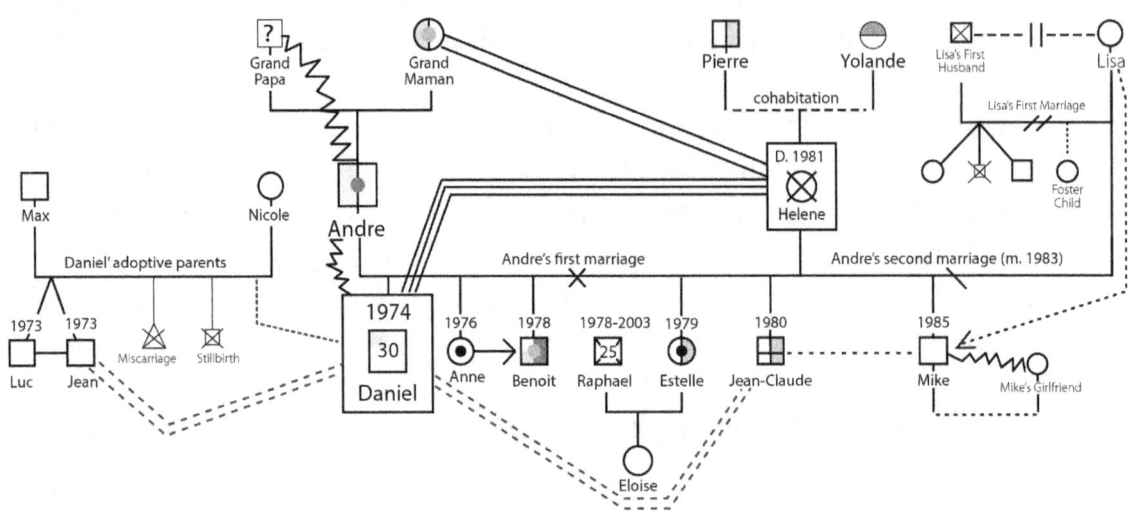

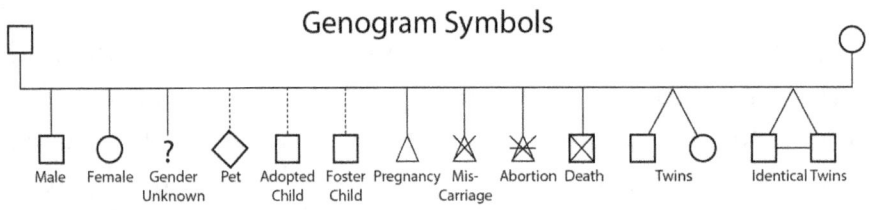

Cognitive Behavioral Therapy

Overview

Cognitive Behavioral Therapy (CBT) is a widely used model within the family therapy field with roots in social cognition research. It is based on the idea that behaviors, cognitive processes, and affect influence dyadic patterns between people. Skills such as couple communication skills are highly emphasized in this form of therapy.

Basic assumptions of CBT include:

❖ Behavior is maintained by its consequences. *Reinforcers* are consequences that accelerate behavior, and consequences that decelerate behavior are called "punishers."

- ❖ There is an intrinsic, unbreakable connection between cognitions, emotions, and behaviors. Specifically, it is believed that negative cognitions can influence behaviors in a cyclical pattern, with cognitions influencing behaviors, and those behaviors influencing cognitions, creating a loop of negative cognitions and behaviors. Negative cognitions and behaviors then help create and contribute to distress and conflict for clients.

- ❖ People's interpretation of the behavior of others affects the way they respond.

- ❖ Automatic thoughts are influenced by cognitive schemas (see below for definition).

Cognitive Behavioral Therapy is widely utilized in the family therapy field for couples using the above-mentioned principles. **Enhanced Cognitive-Behavioral Therapy** for couples represents an expanded version of the classic Cognitive-Behavioral Therapy model used with couples. This enhanced model expands upon these factors to include emphases on:

- ❖ "Broad patterns and core themes in intimate relationships"

- ❖ "Personal characteristics of the two individuals who comprise the couple"

- ❖ "The couple's interactions with their interpersonal and physical environment"

- ❖ "Developmental changes in the partners and relationship to which the couple must adapt"

The primary goal and therapist's role within Enhanced Cognitive-Behavioral Therapy for couples is to teach couples how their cognitions, affect, behaviors, and emotions contribute to their relationship dynamics and quality. This is achieved through a variety of interventions aimed at increasing relationship functionality: cognitive interventions, behavioral interventions, and emotional interventions. Emotion plays a role equivalent to behaviors and cognitions in the enhanced model. This model also recognizes and attempts to increase couples' strengths and social resources more so than the previous classic model.

Leading Figures

- Ivan Pavlov
- B.F. Skinner
- Joseph Wolpe
- Albert Ellis
- Albert Bandura
- Aaron Beck
- Richard Stuart
- Gerald Patterson
- Robert Liberman
- Donald Baucom
- Norman Epstein
- Frank Dattilio

Key Concepts

- **Affect:** One's display of emotion

- **Behaviors:** The actions that one takes

- **Cognitions:** One's thought processes

- **Cognitive distortions:** Errors in one's thought processes; common distortions used in CBT include:

  o **All or nothing thinking:** Viewing matters in rigid categories (e.g., "My imperfect score means I'm a failure"). Also called black and white or **dichotomous thinking**.

  o **Overgeneralization:** Viewing an isolated event that is negative as a persistent pattern of defeat.

  o **Mental filter:** Fixating on one negative detail and excluding any positive details.

- **Disqualifying the positive:** Insisting that positive experiences don't count; this helps maintain a negative belief system that may actually be contradicted by everyday experiences.

- **Jumping to conclusions:** Interpreting a situation in a negative way despite a lack of definite facts to support the negative conclusion. Also called **arbitrary inference**.

- **Mind-reading:** Arbitrarily assuming a negative reaction from someone without confirmation from this person.

- **Magnification (catastrophizing) and minimization (the 'binocular trick'):** Exaggerating the importance of things or inappropriately shrinking things until they appear small (e.g., own self-worth). Also called **selective abstraction**.

- **The fortune teller error:** Expecting that bad things will happen and feeling strongly persuaded that negative predictions are factually-based.

- **Should statements:** Trying to motivate one's self with statements like "I should get in better shape!" The emotional consequence of such statements is often guilt, or anger and resentment, when such statements are directed at others.

- **Emotional reasoning:** Concluding that negative emotions necessarily offer a reflection of reality.

- **Labeling and mislabeling:** An excessive method of overgeneralizing. For example, calling one's self a "loser" or a "big failure."

- **Personalization:** Viewing one's self as the cause of some negative external event, which, in fact, was not one's responsibility.

❖ **Cognitive schemas:** Core beliefs about the world and how it functions; necessary for functioning and not always negative. Related to this are **automatic thoughts**, which are arbitrary and immediate inferences and beliefs that we bring into situations, often unconsciously.

Therapy

CBT's primary goals are to decrease aversive interactions for family members and increase rewarding interactions, teach communication and problem-solving skills to promote healthier interactions, resolve presenting problems, and prevent future problems. Assessment often involves formal tools such as questionnaires and informal tools such as observation. Through questioning, therapists using CBT develop a functional analysis of the inner experiences of clients (thoughts, attitudes, expectations, and beliefs) and which events, thoughts, emotions, and behaviors are causing problems. Evaluating the results of CBT involves assessing the extent to which presenting complaints are resolved, skills are adapted and utilized, and clients are able to correct their own problematic behaviors and thought processes.

CBT interventions include:

- ❖ **Adaptive self-statements:** These challenge automatic thoughts, which are often negative and counterbalance the emotional effects of cognitions. To help develop these, a therapist can:

    o Have a client record thoughts in a stressful situation
    o Have a client discuss which thoughts may contribute to symptoms
    o Come up with strategies for appropriate alternative statements

- ❖ **Altering cognitions:** This involves helping a client alter negative or unproductive thoughts (e.g., cognitive distortions) into healthier, more useful thoughts. To help accomplish this, a therapist may have a client:

    o Identify maladaptive behaviors
    o Identify logical errors that allow maladaptive cognitions to persist
    o Change underlying assumptions

- ❖ **Behavior modification:** Replacing an unwanted behavior with a more desirable one by identifying eliciting cues, specifying a new behavior, and then rewarding progress toward the goal.

- ❖ **Desensitization:** Used to reduce feelings of anxiety, anger, etc. This method involves eliciting negative feelings, or recalling things that induce negative feelings, while in a relaxed state.

- ❖ **Homework:** Often assigned to clients in CBT; relevant to the topic discussed in therapy sessions (e.g., communication skills practice).

- ❖ **Thought-stopping:** A technique for interrupting repetitive cognitions (e.g., shouting to one's self or snapping a rubber band on one's wrist).

- ❖ **Problem-solving:** A skill used in CBT to help clients learn how to resolve their own problems. Steps include:
    - Defining the problem
    - Dividing it into manageable parts
    - Thinking of solutions (and discarding old solutions that did not prove successful in the past)
    - Carrying out the new solution(s)
    - Selecting the best solution(s),
    - Examining the result
    - Modifying the solution at a later time, if necessary

Contextual Therapy

Overview

Contextual Therapy is a systemic model that centers primarily on four relationship dimensions:

- ❖ **First dimension:** The facts of people's lives, like localities, health conditions, and marital status.

- ❖ **Second dimension:** Psychology, which is described as the cognitive and emotional attributes that individuals assign to facts in their lives.

- **Third dimension:** Transactions or family relationship patterns.

- **Fourth dimension:** Relational ethics, considered to be the most important influence that shapes how families exist and operate.

Within this model, it is believed that family members strive to promote fairness by unconsciously forming ties and loyalties with other members by giving out what is owed to certain people and by expecting what is owed to them. Peoples' conflicting inner voices are personified as "parts" and then reintegrated using a variety of "psychodramatic" techniques. Conflicts are often based on polarizations of what one feels, with the assumption that people in conflict with others are often in conflict with themselves and that on the relational level, parts of one family member trigger reactions in parts of other members.

Leading Figures

- Ivan Boszormenyi-Nagy

Key Concepts

- **Filial loyalty:** The inherent loyalty that children are often expected to have toward their parents. For example, "repaying" one's parents by caring for them in their old age.

- **Relational ethics:** The balance of equality and fairness among those with which one has relationships.

- **Revolving slate of injustice:** Transgenerational process in which destructive entitlements (inherent rights) are passed from one generation to another.

- **Transgenerational entitlements/indebtedness:** The expected rights of children within families inherent to being born and of parents within families as the result of children displaying loyalty to them. **Ledgers** are thought to be maintained by individual members of what is owed to them within the family based on ideas of fairness and entitlement.

Therapy

A key goal of the Contextual Therapy approach is to balance fairness among all members of a family. Assessment occurs throughout therapy and is primarily geared toward identifying the four above-mentioned relational dimensions among all family members. A major intervention used is **multidirectional partiality** whereby the therapist sides with each member of the family throughout the therapy process as a way of fostering each member's personal growth and responsibility in family relational patterns. Evaluation of progress is based on members' perceptions of the balance within the family with respect to their own sense of fairness and to how well the system meets their needs.

Emotionally Focused Therapy

Overview

Emotionally Focused Therapy (EFT) is an experiential model based on attachment theory, which considers marital and relationship distress the result of insecure bonds and unfulfilled attachment needs. People are thought to have underlying primary emotions, which are often masked by secondary emotions. These primary emotions represent attachment needs. Likewise, the negative interactional positions that partners within couple relationships assume, "pursuer-distancer," for example, also represent attachment needs. EFT is often used in couples therapy. Key assumptions underlying the model are:

- ❖ The most appropriate paradigm for adult intimacy is that of an emotional bond.

- ❖ Emotion organizes attachment behaviors and the way the self and others are experienced.

- ❖ Problems are sustained by the organization of interactions and each partner's central emotional experience.

- ❖ Desires of partners and attachment needs are essentially adaptive and healthy.

- ❖ Change comes from accessing and reprocessing emotional experience.

Leading Figures

- ❖ Susan Johnson
- ❖ Leslie Greenberg

Key Concepts

- ❖ **Attachment:** The emotional and psychological bond shared with others. Attachment is an innate survival mechanism and a primary motivator for many human social behaviors.

- ❖ **Consolidation:** This involves the crystallization and maintenance of the new, more responsive positions both partners will take in their interactions after working with the EFT therapist and of the integration of their changes into their everyday lives. Using consolidation, the therapist's goal is to identify and support healthy, constructive patterns of interaction.

- ❖ **Pursuers:** Those partners who tend to go after their partners (e.g., beginning an argument) and turn down the "emotional heat" in the relationship in order to protect and preserve it (often a sub-conscious process). Common underlying emotions for pursuers include feeling:

    - o Hurt
    - o Alone
    - o Not wanted
    - o Invisible
    - o Isolated
    - o Unimportant
    - o Abandoned
    - o Desperate
    - o Disconnected
    - o Deprived
    - o Angry

- **Withdrawers:** Those partners who tend to turn away from their partners (e.g., by avoiding or leaving arguments) and turn down the "emotional heat" in the relationship in order to protect and preserve it (often a sub-conscious process). Common underlying emotions for withdrawers include feeling:

    o Rejected
    o Inadequate
    o Afraid of failure
    o Overwhelmed
    o Numb (frozen, don't have needs in battle)
    o Afraid
    o Scared
    o Unwanted, undesirable
    o Judged, criticized
    o Shame
    o Empty
    o Angry

- Other key concepts of EFT are contained in the "Key Techniques" section below.

Therapy

The main goals of Emotionally Focused Therapy are to reveal underlying primary emotions and create new emotional experiences for people. Indeed, emotion is considered the primary agent of change within EFT. For couples, therapeutic change is accomplished primarily by recreating and expanding the emotional experiences between partners, producing new interactions (e.g., shifting partners from desperate blaming to a sense of understanding each other), and promoting secure attachments and bonding. The therapist helps couples stay within their present emotional experience, and within these experiences, the therapist uncovers how each partner individually processes/constructs his/her emotional experiences and looks at how the partners interact with one another during these experiences. Assessment within EFT involves the therapist delineating the couple's core struggle's conflict issues by:

- Assessing the nature of the problem and the relationship – this primarily involves assessing partners' interactional positions, primary and secondary emotions, and attachment histories (e.g., attachment with parents).

- ❖ Beginning to understand how the problem(s) evolved for the couple.

- ❖ Making hypotheses about vulnerabilities and attachment issues.

- ❖ Tracking and describing sequences of interactions – the therapist focuses especially on typical behavior sequences that seem to define the relationship and reflect attachment issues. The sequences of interaction are then plotted from the narrative presentation of the relationship, from the description of specific incidents, and from observations of interactions within sessions.

Emotionally Focused Therapy for couples proceeds in nine general steps:

1. Assess
2. Recognize negative attachment/cycle struggles
3. Retrieve underlying attachment emotions
4. Frame the problem(s) in terms of the interaction cycle and unmet attachment needs
5. Identify implicit fears, needs, and models of self
6. Encourage acceptance of partners by each other
7. Structure emotional engagement
8. Consolidate new positions and interaction cycles; enact new stories
9. Create new solutions to pragmatic issues

Some of the key techniques include:

- ❖ **Alliance-building:** Aim is to create an alliance where both partners feel safe and accepted by the therapist and begin to have confidence that the therapist understands their goals/needs and will be able to help them.

- ❖ **Blamer-softening:** Occurs when the more active and previously hostile spouse risks expressing his/her own vulnerabilities and attachment needs, opening up the opportunity for interactions that confront the relationship's level of trust.

- **Cycle de-escalation:**
    - **First-order change:** The organization of interactions remains the same, but the cycle's elements change somewhat. A couple may begin to initiate some close contact such as lovemaking, seem to find their engagement in therapy reassuring, and begin to be hopeful about their relationship.
    - **Second-order change:** The couple's more hostile partner starts to become less angry and reactive, while the more withdrawn partner becomes more risky regarding engagement in the relationship. These constitute a change in the structure of the relationship.

- **Emphatic interpretation:** This urges one of the partners to expand on his/her present experience, inferring from the therapist's relational context or experience of the person, in order to process his/her experience one step further.

- **Empathic reflection:** This involves the therapist giving reflections of each partner's experience of the relationship and of sequences of interaction, both positive and negative, that characterize the interaction.

- **Evocative responding:** The client's experience and the partial, tentative, or "in process" edges of the experience is the therapist's focus. They invite the client to use one singular experience and to continue processing it, allowing new elements to emerge, and then reorder the experience. This may be done by repeating certain phrases, offering images or metaphors, or asking exploratory questions. Example: "(Wife), what is it like for you to always be walking on eggshells? How does that feel for you?"

- **Heightening:** The therapist must intensify, crystallize, and encourage the couple to enact key problem(s) that organize interactional positions.

- **Reframing:** Providing an alternative, more positive way to view a client's problems or behaviors. A technique in which the given meaning and views of a situation are changed within one's mind without changing the facts (which are usually unchangeable anyway) of a situation. This is used early on, on a relatively superficial level in

EFT with couples. For example, in the first session, the therapist may begin to frame one spouse as deprived and the other as needing to protect the self through distance. However, this depends on whether the partners express their experience in a way that is amenable to such formulations. Such reframes can be incorporated as part of the description of the cycle. Example: "The moving away is your way of standing up for yourself, protecting yourself from his 'poking', yes? And for you, poking is your way of saying, 'I'm here, here I am, let me in, see me.' Is that it?"

- **Validation:** Therapist conveys the message that partners' emotions and responses are legitimate and understandable, and their responses are the best solutions they could find in light of each partner's experience of the relationship. This proactive acceptance of each person is essential in creating a strong alliance and to the process of EFT.

- **Withdrawer engagement:** The more withdrawn partner begins to become more active and engaged in the relationship. This shift involves a change in an interactional position, specifically with control and openness to connection. This partner begins to assert his/her needs and wants instead of shutting down or avoiding the spouse and becomes more emotionally engaged with his/her partner in therapy sessions.

Experiential Therapy

Overview

Experiential Therapy is a humanistic, experiential approach to treating families. Emotional expression is valued over intellectual reasoning to help clients achieve change including becoming more expressive, having more fulfillment in their roles, and being more genuine with one another. The underlying assumptions about human nature include the following:

- People want to increase their abilities to be sensitive and genuine with each other, although the strategies they use sometimes to achieve these goals are flawed.

- Low self-esteem blocks people's ability to share their emotional experiences, resulting in dysfunctional family relationships.

- Families that are not in touch with the present are "emotionally dead."

Leading Figures

- Virginia Satir
- Carl Whitaker
- Walter Kempler
- Fred Duhl
- Bunny Duhl
- Peggy Papp
- David Kantor

Key Concepts

- **Here-and-now experience**: The present, immediate experience; the emphasis for producing new experiences for family members within therapy.

- Five main patterns – sometimes called **"poses"** or **"communication stances"** – used by people to cope with emotions. The first four are considered those that help people hide their feelings and thus are considered maladaptive:

  o **Placating:** Involves pacifying others, glossing over differences, and acting defensive of others when conflict arises. "Placators" are thought to be outwardly agreeable, but inwardly disagreeable.

  o **Blaming:** Involves being judgmental of others and comparing and/or complaining when conflict arises. "Blamers" are thought to be outwardly domineering, but inwardly insecure.

  o **Computing:** Involves using logic, lecturing, and outside authority when conflict arises. "Computers" are thought to be outwardly immobile and inwardly vulnerable.

- o **Distracting:** Also called avoiding, this stance involves changing the subject, pretending not to understand, being quiet, and pretending to be weak and helpless when conflict arises. "Distracters" are thought to appear in constant motion on the outside and inwardly alienated.

- o **Leveling:** Also called being congruent, this stance involves displaying affect and behavior consistent and appropriate to a given situation. "Levelers" are thought to be those who are the "real" and authentic responders and emotionally "alive."

Therapy

A therapist using Experiential Therapy is a facilitator and coach for families, as well as a "gentle challenger," promoting more positive, authentic experiences. This model focuses on clients' strengths, not their pathologies. Therapy involves helping family members realize which of the "poses" they are using and creating a safe space for them to reveal their true feelings. Key techniques include:

❖ **Family art therapy (conjoint family drawing):** The therapist asks family members to create drawing that portray the family's organizational structure. Family art therapy also sometimes involves a joint family scribble, in which the whole family produces a unified picture from scribbles drawn by each member.

❖ **Family sculpture (relationship sculpture or space sculpture):** The therapist asks family members to symbolically depict events and processes by organizing one another into tables. This technique illuminate past incidents and be insightful because it helps to unblock and demonstrate emotions or extricate emotions. The therapist can offer direction toward preferred alternatives with the information gained from this exercise.

❖ **Role-playing:** Clients act out events and recollections from the past and hoped-for future events in order to make the events more emotionally real and present.

❖ **Symbolic drawing of life space:** Families portray communication patterns and emotional distance with symbolic drawings. Family members arrange people in and around a large circle, demonstrating whether each person is a part of the family or not.

- ❖ **The empty chair technique:** A Gestalt therapy technique, which involves having a client speak to an empty chair as if he/she were speaking to a particular family member who is not present in the session. The goal of this technique is to encourage an individual to own the feelings/beliefs that he/she has been projecting onto others.

Assessment within Experiential Therapy is unstructured and involves searching for suppressed feelings, impulses of family members, and family members' processes (ways of relating to one another).

Narrative Therapy

Overview

Narrative Therapy is an approach to family therapy whereby family members are encouraged to evaluate their stories or "narratives" about their experiences and to alter any unhealthy stories that may keep the client or family stuck in destructive patterns. Problems such as eating disorders are treated as external factors and not as personal attributes of any particular family member. This theoretical approach is based on the assumption that individuals and families maintain "narratives" or dominating stories about their lives. These stories are a combination of both fact and fiction, as people often remember not only the facts of past events, but "narrative truths" as well to help make sense of the past. In other words, clients create stories for their lives that influence their perceptions of reality. It is believed that many individuals and families maintain **problem-saturated stories**, which keep problems alive.

Leading Figures

- ❖ Gene Combs
- ❖ Jill Freedman
- ❖ David Epston
- ❖ Michael White
- ❖ Jeffrey Zimmerman
- ❖ Vicki Dickerson
- ❖ Stephan Madigan

- ❖ Kathe Weingarten
- ❖ Sallyann Roth
- ❖ Harlene Anderson
- ❖ Harry Goolishan

Key Concepts

- ❖ **Deconstruction:** Exploring and breaking apart the unproductive narratives that clients share and helping them adopt healthier ones that promote change; the eventual goal is helping clients re-author their **dominant stories** and then reinforcing the re-authored dominant stories.

- ❖ **Dominant story:** A client's principal view of the world.

- ❖ **Problem-saturated stories:** Narratives that are generally negative and fixed and include a narrow focus on problems; such narratives are thought to be the key factor that keeps clients "stuck."

Therapy

The goal of Narrative Therapy is to reveal the unhelpful stories in clients' lives and replace them with more positive ones. Assessment is generally not formal, but rather, involves deconstruction (described above) and exploring unique outcomes (described below). The techniques that therapists use to help clients reach their goals include:

- ❖ **Externalizing problems:** The problem is defined as an outside force to the family, which all members can work against. Particular clients or family members are not considered the problem, but instead, some force external to the client or family is considered the problem.

- ❖ **Exploring unique outcomes:** These are past times in which family members were able to act positively in the face of their problems and resolve them (similar to the concept of **past exceptions** in Solution-Focused Therapy).

- ❖ **Letter-writing:** May be done by both clients and therapists; types of letters used include:

- o **Letters of invitation:** Written by the therapist and family members to invite a reluctant member to come to therapy.

- o **Letters of prediction:** Usually written by the therapist and sent to the family after therapy; expresses the therapist's positive predictions for the family regarding their progress after the conclusion of therapy.

- ❖ **Reflecting team:** Sometimes used in Narrative Therapy, this is a team of several therapists who observe family sessions and share their reactions with the family following a session.

- ❖ **Relative influence questions:** Questions designed to explore when a problem has control or when clients perceive that they do.

- ❖ **Strengthening social support:** Improving a client or family's network of people who support their goals and healthy development.

Object Relations Therapy

Overview

Object Relations Therapy is based on object relations theory, which stems from psychoanalytic theory. The theory's focus is on psychoanalysis, or uncovering deep motives that drive people's behavior and thoughts. This type of therapy tends to be long-term compared to other types within family therapy, with treatment sometimes lasting several years. Some assumptions underlying Object Relations Therapy include:

- ❖ The basic human motive is the search for satisfying relationships with other humans.

- ❖ Unconscious forces from childhood determine the behavioral patterns that develop in adulthood and in adult relationships.

- ❖ Intrapsychic pathology commonly appears as relationship distress.

Leading Figures

- ❖ Melanie Klein
- ❖ Ronald Fairbairn
- ❖ Donald Winnicot
- ❖ James Framo
- ❖ Norman Paul
- ❖ David Scharff
- ❖ Jill Scharff

Key Concepts

- ❖ **False self:** The idea that we hide some of our own needs and feelings in order to win approval. For example, children tend to suppress feelings they fear may lead to rejection (e.g., behaving as if they are "perfect angels").

- ❖ **Good-enough parenting:** The average expectable environment that a parent can provide to a child. For example, providing an environment in which an infant can reliably predict what is going to happen (e.g., if I am hungry and cry, I will be fed).

- ❖ **Idealization:** The model that parents offer to a child, which can help them have positive beliefs about his/her parents and in turn himself/herself (e.g., "my father/mother is a good, strong person, and I am part of him/her" may lead to a firm base of self-esteem).

- ❖ **Internal objects:** The mental images a person has of himself/herself and of others, which are based on experiences and expectations developed over time.

- ❖ **Insight:** The process used to produce change.

- ❖ **Introjects:** Imprints (repressed memories) of parents or other significant figures.

- ❖ **Mirroring:** The process of a parent validating a child and letting him/her know that he/she is understood and accepted.

- ❖ **Projective identification:** Unconscious defense mechanism. Undesirable characteristics of self are assigned to another who is incited to act according to the projected feelings.

- ❖ **Splitting:** A coping mechanism employed to reduce anxiety whereby the idea of "good-object" and "bad-object" develop around internal objects.

Therapy

In general, the goals of Object Relations Therapy are to provide clients with insight and work through intrapsychic struggles that affect clients' interactions with others and developmental phases. Assessment is not structured and may take place throughout therapy as a therapist guides a client toward increased insight and develops ideas about his/her objects and related conflicts. The main techniques used by a therapist within this model include:

- ❖ **Empathic listening:** Concerted attention to detect latent meaning behind speech or interactions.

- ❖ **Interpretation:** The therapist offers the client a subjective meaning or motive behind a reported or observed behavior, affect, or opinion.

- ❖ **Transference:** A client's feelings, drives, attitudes, and fantasies being unconsciously shifted onto the therapist; these aspects are displaced from unresolved emotions regarding significant persons from the past of the client.

- ❖ **Countertransference:** The analysis of spontaneous reactions toward a client's transference; considered a vital source of information about intrapsychic deficits. This involves the therapist's unconscious emotional responses to a client that are reminiscent of feelings he/she experienced with a person in the past.

Psychoanalytic Family Therapy

Overview

Psychoanalytic Family Therapy has roots dating back to the work of Sigmund Freud who theorized that people move through stages of psychosexual development across their lifespan and are driven by sexual and aggressive drives. The original focus of this theory within families was on neurotic individuals, as it was believed that mental disorders such as schizophrenia developed in response to family problems, particularly "defective" mothers. The idea developed that there existed "schizophrenogenic mothers" who were domineering, aggressive, rejecting, and insecure, providing the basis for the development of disorders in their children. Born out of this model of family therapy is Object Relations Therapy (see section "Object Relations Therapy" for a detailed description).

The assumptions of Psychoanalytic Family Therapy include the following:

- ❖ Neuroses stem from childhood conflicts that were generated by colliding forces of inner drives and external experiences.

- ❖ Our innate drives form the basis for understanding a person's motivation, conflicts, and symptomatic behavior.

- ❖ Family relationships impact an individual's character formation (i.e. symptomatic behavior).

Leading Figures

- ❖ Sigmund Freud
- ❖ Carl Jung
- ❖ Erik Erikson
- ❖ Adelaide Johnson
- ❖ Nathan Ackerman
- ❖ Erich Fromm
- ❖ Henry Dicks
- ❖ Alfred Adler
- ❖ Harry Stack Sullivan
- ❖ Karen Horney

Key Concepts

- ❖ **Defense mechanisms:** Unconscious ego device a person calls on for protection against anxiety.

- ❖ **Phobia:** Fear displaced into a substitute object.

- ❖ **Projections:** An unconscious defense mechanism in which unwanted aspects of one's self are credited to the person who is incited to act according to the projected feelings.

Therapy

The general goal of Psychoanalytic Family Therapy is to tap into the unconscious constrictions of family members so that interactions may become healthier. More specifically, the goals are to create individual intrapsychic change, resolve family pathogenic conflict, promote detriangulation between members (i.e., removing third parties from conflict between two people), promote the removal of projections, and increase levels of individuation (i.e., psychological separation and independence from others). The therapist is to remain neutral and conduct an unstructured assessment, which may last throughout the course of therapy. A therapist may seek answers to these five questions, offered by Arnon Bentovim and Warren Kinston, for the purposes of assessment:

1. "What is the effect of the symptom on the family dynamics? What is the effect of familial interactions on the symptom?"

2. "What is the current symptom's function?"

3. "Is there some fear preventing the family from addressing their conflicts in the best way possible?"

4. "In what way is the present issue associated with prior trauma?"

5. "What summary could the therapist summarize provide regarding the focal conflict?"

Some key techniques that may be employed to help improve individual and family functioning include:

- ❖ **Analytic neutrality:** Understanding without worrying about solving problems.

- ❖ **Empathy:** Not advising, reassuring, or confronting, but understanding clients' experience from their position.

- ❖ **Interpretations:** Clarifying hidden aspects (e.g., primary motives) of clients' experience by interpreting their statements and behaviors.

- ❖ **Listening:** Not feeling pressured to do something, but rather, to just listen as clients share.

In Psychoanalytic Family Therapy, since it is believed that insight leads to understanding, conflict reduction, and ultimately, individual intrapsychic change, as well as family system change, evaluation of therapy results is not as clear-cut as in other models of family therapy, and there are various opinions about how to best evaluate the results of this type of therapy. Possible ways include examining clients' reactions to see if they are healthier (although this is open to subjective interpretation) and exploring if the insights of a client have been expanded upon.

Strategic Therapy

Overview

Strategic Therapy is a model of family therapy that was born out of communication theory. According to communication theory, there are two general theories of change including the "Theory of Groups" and the "Theory of Logical Types." Both of these theories are abstract and are pulled from mathematical logic concepts. The "Theory of Groups" involves change that occurs *within* a human system without changing of the system itself, also called a first-order change. The "Theory of Logical Types" involves second-order change, or change that occurs directly *to* a human system such that the entire system is transformed and reshaped. Second-order change is considered crucial to achieving long-term change, although it can often be the most difficult type of change for many families to make. With second-order change, the solutions come from outside the actual system and often appear impossible or illogical to group members within the system.

Strategic Therapy is focused on solutions for handling **difficulties** (considered distinct and less severe than **problems**), which often contribute to the formation and maintenance of many problems. The underlying assumption is that people and families often mishandle difficulties, thus leading to problems. This is thought to occur in three main ways:

1. People may deny the existence of difficulties.

2. Change may be attempted when it is impossible or when difficulties do not exist and change is not needed.
3. People may make errors in logical typing by attempting to apply the wrong type of change to difficulties; specifically, first-order change may be applied when second-order change is necessary, or vice versa.

To simplify these fallacies in the handling of difficulties, action may be needed, but none is taken; no action may be needed, and some is taken; or action may be needed and taken, but at the wrong logical level of change.

There are three distinct models of Strategic Therapy, all of which stem from communication theory:

- Jay Haley and Cloe Madanes' Strategic Therapy
- Milan Systemic Family Therapy
- MRI Brief Therapy (developed at the Mental Research Institute in Palo Alto, California)

Leading Figures

- Gregory Bateson
- Cloe Madanes
- Jay Haley
- Don Jackson
- William Fry
- Paul Watzlawick
- John Weakland
- Richard Fisch
- Karl Tomm
- Milton Erickson
- Mara Selvini Palazzoli

Key Concepts

Key concepts within each of the models of Strategic Therapy include:

- ❖ **Circular causality:** The idea that problems do not have linear causes.

- ❖ **Cybernetics:** The study of how information processing systems use feedback loops to self-correct. Feedback loops are the mechanisms or cycles of interactions through which information is returned to the system and exerts an influence on it. Negative feedback loops promote homeostasis, or the maintenance of the status quo, within family systems; positive feedback loops promote deviation from the status quo and change within family systems.

Therapy

In **Haley and Madanes' Strategic Therapy**, the goal is for family members to change their behaviors and have different experiences. Techniques within Haley and Madanes' Strategic Therapy include:

- ❖ **Directives:** Tasks assigned in therapy that may involve part or all of the family. These are concise and typically start with in the session and continue at home. Like all strategic therapies, the problem's sequences are tracked by the therapist who assigns directives that alter the sequence. Directives aim to correct dysfunctional hierarchies by modifying family structure and strengthening the parental unit.

- ❖ **Pretend techniques:** Encouraging clients (e.g., children) to pretend to have their symptoms and those around them (e.g., parents) to pretend to help. This highlights the control that family members have over symptoms.

- ❖ **Ordeals:** Making it more difficult for a client to maintain a symptom than it is to give it up by prescribing certain tasks around the symptom.

Milan Systemic Family Therapy is a pragmatic, brief therapy, orchestrated by the therapist. The therapy aims to interrupt behavior patterns that are maintaining problems. Change occurs when the therapist actively intervenes to alter the family's typical interactional patterns (shifting the ways that the family members respond to each other). Therapists are encouraged to be direct, warm, engaging, flexible, and creative and are considered an active agent who joins the family in a personal relationship. Techniques include:

- **Therapy teams** composed of two members (originally male-female co-therapists) were formed to provide families with the following:
    - "Pre-session: Initial hypothesis formed by the team"
    - "Session: Hypothesis modified or validated"
    - "Intersession: Intervention during meeting of the team"
    - "Intervention: Positive connotation or ritual and a rule against change"
    - "Post-session discussion: Team session reflection and plan formulation"

- **Positive connotation:** Associating a family member's behavior with a positive value or motive.

- **Rituals:** Validate a positive connotation or obligate family's exaggeration or violation of family rules.

- **Invariant prescription:** Parents form a secret coalition.

- **Circular questioning:** A technique used to help families discover the systemic nature of their relational patterns in that the questions posed require responses in relational terms. The main purpose for this type of questioning is to give families a new perspective, specifically a cyclical viewpoint, of their presenting problems. Therapists who use this technique are expected to remain neutral, form hypotheses about the family and their presenting problem, and make use of circularity in both the exploration and intervention phases of cases. The circular questions themselves are categorized across four different dimensions:
    - Problem definition
    - Sequence of interaction
    - Comparison/classification
    - Intervention

Within each of these categories, therapists should gather information from families on the present, the past, and the future regarding their interaction patterns. All families are unique, and therapists utilizing circular questions should tailor them to individual families, remain flexible, and be creative during the process.

- ❖ **Odd day/even day ritual:** Assignment for clients to act one way on odd days, another way on even days, and spontaneous on the 7th day.

- ❖ **Therapeutic neutrality:** Assuming that a system in its entirety ought to be given equal focus.

In **MRI Brief Therapy**, rather than a focus on normative patterns of development or family health criteria, therapists focus on techniques for change. Also, rather than a focus on family structure, therapists analyze faulty cycles of interaction, motivated by erroneous problem-solving efforts. Therapy within MRI Brief Therapy proceeds in six steps:

1. Outline the organization of treatment.

2. Identification and examination of the issue.

3. Hypothesis of the behaviors sustaining the issue.

4. Establishing treatment goals and exploring previous attempts to solve the problem. Of the three general solutions a family might consider, each offers a specific intervention strategy:

    1. If they have *denied*, encourage them to *act*.
    2. If they have *tried to solve* a nonexistent problem, encourage them to *stop acting*.
    3. If they have *taken the wrong action*, encourage them to *take a different action*.

5. Picking a behavioral intervention and employing it.
6. Termination.

The key techniques within MRI Brief Therapy include:

- ❖ **Reframing:** Providing an alternative, more positive way to view a client's problems or behavior.

- **Paradoxical interventions:** Recommending seemingly counterproductive activity for treatment. (Note: This may be seen as deceptive by some therapists.) Types include the following:

  - **"Devil's Pact":** The therapist gains the compliance of his/her client to follow his/her instructions before the client is actually told what he/she should do. Considered a useful way for therapists to combat the frequent problem of their clients rejecting change because of its perceived difficulty or inconvenience.

  - **Positioning:** The therapist convinces the family to minimize a problem by exaggerating it, instigating the family to disagree.

  - **Restraining techniques:** The therapist associates himself/herself with the ambivalence of resisting change, which encourages the family seek change. The therapist achieves this by warning the family members of change's dangers, restricting change altogether or limiting it to a slow rate.

  - **Symptom prescription:** The therapist recommends that the family continue or even increase their performance of the symptom. If the therapists wants the family to perform the action, it is considered compliance-based, while the directive is defiance-based when he/she aims for the family to defy it.

Sex Therapy

Overview

Sex Therapy is a form of family therapy designed to treat issues surrounding human sexuality. These may include sexual dysfunction, sexual disorders, or intimacy and desire problems. Sex Therapy is generally performed using behaviorally focused models such as Cognitive Behavioral Therapy.

Leading Figures

- William Masters
- Virginia Johnson

Key Concepts

Some key concepts involved in Sex Therapy include:

- **Dyspareunia:** Painful intercourse.

- **Organic sexual dysfunction:** Impaired sexual functioning that has physiological causes (e.g., chronic illness).

- **Psychosexual sexual dysfunction:** Impaired sexual functioning that has psychological causes (e.g., performance anxiety).

- **Female arousal disorder:** May involve inadequate lubrication or genital swelling during the excitement phase of sex.

- **Female orgasmic disorder:** Inability to orgasm during sex. Since many women do not experience orgasms, this disorder should be given cautiously and with very thorough assessment on the part of the therapist.

- **Male erectile disorder (impotence):** Inability to have or sustain an erection.

- **Spectatoring:** A cognitive process that is the tendency to monitor one's sexual performance; often contributes to sexual dysfunction and may be preceded by performance anxiety.

Therapy

The goal of Sex Therapy is to resolve issues related to sex and intimacy for clients. Therapists may elect to use a major MFT model to treat clients for such issues, while using techniques specific to Sex Therapy to help clients reach their goals. When conducting assessment and interviews during Sex Therapy, therapists ought to be aware that clients may have difficulties discussing sex, may not use correct terminology, or may be uneducated about sexual issues (e.g., sexual functioning). It is critical to collect psychosexual and psychosocial history during Sex Therapy interviews, display sensitivity for hidden issues, and provide a second opportunity for disclosure of relevant information. Also, it is good idea to refer any client who has not recently had a medical exam or describes symptoms such as pain or bleeding to a physician for a medical evaluation as a part of his/her therapy assessment. Along with a standard medical history form, useful Sex Therapy assessment instruments include:

- ❖ Derogatis Sexual Functioning Inventory
- ❖ Brief Index of Sexual Functioning for Women
- ❖ HIV Knowledge Questionnaire
- ❖ International Index of Erectile Function
- ❖ Inventory of Dyadic Heterosexual Preferences
- ❖ Sexual Desire Inventory
- ❖ Sexual Opinion Survey

Challenges that may complicate assessment within Sex Therapy include uncooperative partners, single clients with no partners, and patients abusing alcohol or other drugs.

Key techniques within Sex Therapy include:

- ❖ **Sensate focus:** A desensitization technique aimed at helping clients lower anxiety levels, decrease focus on distractions such as performance, and increase focus on the pleasurable sensations of sex while staying present with their partner. It is a structured approach, but allows for some flexibility. It produces change gradually over time and involves home exercises, which are carried out between therapy sessions. If done correctly, sensate focus can help partners broaden their approaches to sexual interactions, alter perceptions of one another, and open the lines of communication surrounding sexual issues.

    o General procedure:

    - Non-genital pleasuring and touching while partners are dressed
    - Genital pleasuring
    - Containment with no thrusting
    - Thrusting and intercourse

- ❖ **Biomedical interventions:** Medical interventions may be needed for some clients, so it is essential that clients seeking Sex Therapy for issues related to sexual dysfunction are referred to their medical physician for assessment and possible medical treatment (e.g., hormone therapy, medication).

- ❖ **Creating an environment conducive for sex:** Many complaints in Sex Therapy come from partners attempting sexual activities under adverse conditions (e.g., unpleasant surroundings, kids, other distractions). Therapists can help clients identify and alter these conditions.

- ❖ **Cognitive restructuring:** This may include challenging negative attitudes or reducing interfering thoughts; (refer to section "Cognitive Behavioral Therapy" for more on cognitive restructuring).

Solution-Focused Therapy

Overview

The solution-focused approach is a form of brief family therapy founded on the work of Steve de Shazer and Insoo Kim Berg. The MRI model of family therapy is the basis for solution-focused therapy, and the goal is to help clients think, behave, and talk differently about their problems to ultimately achieve more satisfaction with their lives. One advantage of this theoretical model is that it typically has a briefer treatment period than other models of family therapy. Solution-Focused Therapy assumes that people genuinely want to change, but that pessimism and patterns of narrow, unproductive solutions hinder them from their desired change. In other words, clients come to therapy with their own strengths and solutions to problems, but negative cognitions get in the way of effectively enacting solutions. This model addresses cognitions and is future-oriented; solution-focused therapists do not focus on the past or search for the cause of problems.

Leading Figures

- ❖ Insoo Kim Berg
- ❖ Steve de Shazer
- ❖ Eve Lipchik
- ❖ Michele Weiner-Davis
- ❖ Scott Miller
- ❖ John Walter

- Jane Peller
- Bill O'Hanlon
- Yvonne Dolan

Key Concepts

- **Cognitions:** One's thought processes.

- **Exceptions:** Also called *past exceptions*, these are times when clients' problems were not problems because clients applied workable solutions to them. For example, a therapist may ask a client, "When was this problem not a problem?"

- **Future:** Used as a driving force in this form of therapy and considered the time ahead when clients' problems are resolved.

- **Solutions:** The primary focus of this form of therapy.

- Categories of family members based on their stage of change:

    - **Complainant:** Someone who makes a complaint, without putting for the effort to solve the issue. The therapist must engage him/her in the conversation, compliment him/her, and maybe give an assignment to observe exceptions to the problem. The goal here is to turn the client into a **customer**.

    - **Customer:** Someone who is motivated to change.

    - **Visitor:** Someone who is not motivated to change.

Therapy

Solution-Focused Therapy' primary goal is to resolve clients' presenting problems. This is achieved by shifting clients' language and cognitive focus away from problems and the past and towards solutions and the future. A therapist using the solution-focused model uses language carefully to help achieve this. Therapy proceeds in three major phases:

1. Positively reframing problems and highlighting current resources and strengths

2. Clarifying narrow binds in which clients have placed themselves

3. Promoting progress and change through the use of direct, change-oriented behavior.

Assessment involves the therapist gaining an understanding of the patterns of behavior that existed when the problem was not present (i.e., identifying past exceptions). Solution-Focused Therapy techniques include:

- **Clarifying narrow binds:** Identifying negative beliefs and cognitions that keep clients stuck in problems and unable to make needed changes. An example of a narrow bind is a client expressing, "That's just how my life is; it'll never change!" A therapist can help a client see how holding onto this belief works against progress and keeps the client bound to his/her problems.

- **Formula first session task:** Usually assigned after the first session, this is a standard assignment that requires the client to observe things in his/her life before he/she returns to therapy. For example, a therapist may request the client to observe his/her situation in order to elaborate on his/her needs within the context of the marriage, family, life, ect.

- **Joining:** Socializing is the initial process of connecting with the client.

- **Miracle question:** Usually asked early in the therapy process, this question asks clients what would be different in their lives if a miracle were to occur. For example, a therapist may ask what change they would expect to notice if the issue was solved instantaneously and miraculously.

- **Reframe:** An alternative, more positive way to view a client's problems or behavior. A technique in which the given meaning and views of a situation are changed within one's mind without changing the facts (which are usually unchangeable anyway) of a situation.

- **Future-oriented questions:** Questions designed to shift clients away from thinking only of their problems and more toward possible solutions and a better future. Examples include:

    o "What seems to be the current problem?"
    o "What would indicate to you that the problem was resolved?"
    o "How will you know when you no longer need to see me?"
    o "What is your wildest fantasy about what you want to happen?"

- **Scaling:** A technique of having clients quantify and rate their own progress and confidence in solving their problems. A therapist might ask, "On a scale of 1 to 10, how bad do you think your communication is with your partner at this time?" or "On a scale of 1 to 10, how confident are you that you can reach your goal of reconnecting with your former best friend?"

Structural Therapy

Overview

The structural model of therapy was founded by Salvador Minuchin and is based on his work as a child psychiatrist working with delinquent youth. It is centered on the idea that individual people do not exist in social isolation, but rather, within social groups in which they both influence and are influenced by their surroundings, the most immediate of which is the family. Family structure is thought to dictate the behavioral and relational patterns of family members, and inadequate structures within family subsystems result in dysfunctional relational patterns.

Minuchin points out that families across all societies and cultures must deal with life cycle transitions and macro-level changes in which it is normal, not pathological, to experience stresses and strains. According to this model, problems within families often stem from:

- The inadequate parent-child subsystem structure; this subsystem should be hierarchically arranged with the parents at the top of the hierarchy.

- ❖ The homeostatic functions of the family; members often collectively contribute to the maintenance of current relational patterns, even if they are dysfunctional.

- ❖ The inability of the family to adapt to normative and non-normative developmental changes.

Leading Figures

- ❖ Salvador Minuchin
- ❖ Harry Aponte
- ❖ Braulio Montalvo
- ❖ Marianne Walters
- ❖ Dick Auerswald
- ❖ Charlie King
- ❖ Clara Rabinowitz
- ❖ Stephen Greenstein
- ❖ Charles Fishman
- ❖ Carter Umbarger

Key Concepts

The key concepts within the structural framework include:

- ❖ **Boundaries:** Relational barriers that exist around **subsystems**. There are three main types of boundaries, all defined by how penetrable they are:

    o **Clear:** Boundaries that maintain a functional and healthy level of penetrability.

    o **Rigid:** Boundaries that are heavily resistant to outside influences; subsystems with rigid boundaries are often characterized as "disengaged" from the family unit.

    o **Diffuse:** Boundaries that are too easily penetrated, resulting in low levels of autonomy and impaired functioning for the subsystem; subsystems with diffuse boundaries are often characterized as "enmeshed" with the family unit.

- ❖ **Coalition:** The joining of two family members against a third member. These are viewed as "stable" if they remain relatively unchanged within the family's relational interactions and as "detoured" if the two joined members see the third member as the cause of their conflicts.

- ❖ **Enmeshment:** The result of family subsystems in which the members are overly involved with one another, offering little individual autonomy, independence, or competence.

- ❖ **Disengagement:** The result of family subsystems in which the members have limited contact with one another, offering individual autonomy and independence, but resulting in isolation.

- ❖ **Hierarchy:** The rank-based organization of familial subsystems.

- ❖ **Homeostatic functions:** Maintain the status quo within a family system.

- ❖ **Joining:** Establishing a strong therapeutic relationship with the family; a prerequisite to achieving therapeutic goals.

- ❖ **Reframing:** An alternative, more positive way to view a client's problems or behavior. A technique in which the given meaning and views of a situation are changed within one's mind without changing the facts (which are usually unchangeable anyway) of a situation.

- ❖ **Rules:** Regular patterns of interaction to which families adhere; these may be:

    - o **Generic:** Universal relational patterns assumed across all families.

    - o **Idiosyncratic:** Unspoken and implied patterns specific to a particular family.

- ❖ **Subsystem:** A smaller unit within a larger family unit that operates in a regularly established relational pattern and carries out particular roles. There are three main subsystems: spousal, parental, and child/sibling.

The following are common symbols used to diagram family structure:

Rigid boundary ⸻⸻⸻⸻⸻

Clear boundary ---------------------------------

Diffuse boundary ....

Coalition ⌢⌢⌢⌢⌢⌢⌢⌢⌢

Conflict ⸻⊣ ⊢⸻

Detouring ⸻⸻⸻⸻⟶

Involvement ══════════

Over-involvement ≡≡≡≡≡≡≡≡≡≡

The following is an example of these symbols applied to two different example scenarios. The first is parents with enmeshed children, and the second is non-acceptance of a step parent (F stands for father, M stands for mother):

Therapy

The goals of Structural Therapy are to address present issues (with little emphasis on the past), transform the structure of the family system, and emphasize the family's own abilities to functionally adapt to change. To produce therapeutic change, an individual's most crucial context, his/her family, is restructured in a more functional manner. The beginning of therapy involves techniques like gradual **joining** and carefully executed probing, which will help assess and reveal a family's structure and relational patterns. From this, the therapist can begin forming a "family map," or a simplified outline of family transactional patterns. Then, the therapist's role is to work toward helping families restructure dysfunctional patterns and strengthen the parental subsystem. Specific restructuring techniques include what Minuchin terms a "yes, and" approach, in which a therapist works toward the maintenance of subsystems that already contain the capacity for appropriately dealing with change, and a "yes, but" approach, in which new subsystems and relational patterns are formed to promote adaptation to change. In summary, there are three stages of therapy in this approach:

1. Joining/accommodating
2. Structural assessment and diagnosis
3. Restructuring

The progression of therapy can be measured in two ways: a family's steps toward larger therapy goals and the smaller steps of dealing with individual issues as they arise within single sessions. According to Minuchin, the main shortcomings of the structural family therapy model are the inattentiveness to developmental processes and the support of certain family subsystems at the expense of others (Minuchin, 1974). For some, Structural Therapy may also be considered too brief or not thorough enough, as therapy may end after the presenting problem is resolved.

Chapter 2: The Practice of MFT

The following contains major themes related practicing family and marital therapy such as assessment and diagnosis, special duties of therapists, and special practice concerns. Those taking the national MFT exam are expected to have knowledge of these issues.

Assessment Issues

Within marital and family therapy, assessment may take place as early as the first client contact and last as long as throughout the entire course of treatment. MFTs typically assess the following areas:

- ❖ **Presenting concern(s):** It is important to assess this from all family members' points of view. Assessing the presenting problem will help an MFT determine if the issue falls within his/her scope of practice, what type of interventions may be needed, and how long therapy may last.

- ❖ **Family system:** Assessing a family system primarily involves gaining an understanding of who the members are in the family along with how the members define their roles (e.g., father as primary "breadwinner"). This also involves understanding the family structure dynamics such as the presence of triangles or unhealthy boundaries (see section "Structural Therapy" for specific ways to assess family structure).

- ❖ **Family life cycle stage:** As stated earlier, the family life cycle stages are the common stages by which families develop and change across the lifespan (e.g., "leaving home" and "joining of families through marriage"). MFTs are expected to assess which stage their clients are in and use this information to help understand what transition-related problems a given family may be facing and help "normalize" such problems.

- ❖ **Family violence:** MFTs may encounter cases of child abuse, elder abuse, or abuse between domestic partners. MFTs are expected to be aware of signs of such abuse and the appropriateness of family therapy treatment if such abuse is present. In some cases, therapists may need to report such abuse according to state law.

- ❖ **Issues related to culture, gender, and sexual orientation:** MFTs are expected to have knowledge of issues in each of these areas as they relate to providing family therapy. During assessment, it is important to gather information about how these factors shape clients' lives and possibly contribute to their presenting problems. For example, each member of a couple may have different expectations about his/her household roles based on differing gender role expectations, or partners with different ethnic/cultural backgrounds may experience issues related to the blending of different cultural backgrounds or the joining of their families of origin.

- ❖ **Psychopathology:** One or more members of a family may have a mental health disorder or display signs of such a disorder and need proper evaluation. The Diagnostic and Statistical Manual of Mental Disorders (DSM) is the most common assessment tool for diagnosing disorders. More information about the DSM is provided later in this section.

- ❖ **Substance use and abuse:** MFTs should use both informal and formal tools when necessary to assess any issues related to problematic drug or alcohol use and/or abuse. Often times, family therapy interventions are not effective unless substance abuse issues are first resolved.

Assessment and Diagnostic Inventories

The following is a list of standard scales and questionnaires used in marital and family therapy. (Note: This is not an exhaustive list of all such inventories.)

- ❖ Abusive Behavior Inventory
- ❖ Abuse within Intimate Relationships Scale (AIRS)
- ❖ Adolescent Substance Abuse Subtle Screening Inventory (SASSI-A2)
- ❖ Achenbach System of Empirically Based Assessment (ASEBA)
- ❖ Adult-Adolescent Parenting Inventory (AAPI-2)
- ❖ Children's Depression Inventory (CDI)
- ❖ Beck Depression Inventory II (BDI-II)

- Clinical Rating Scale (CRS)
- Composite Abuse Scale (CAS)
- Conners' Rating Scales Revised (CRS-R)
- Conflict Tactics Scales Handbook (CTS)
- Dyadic Adjustment Scale (DAS)
- Family Environment (FES)
- Family Assessment Measure (FAM)
- Family Assessment Device (FAS)
- Family Adaptability and Cohesion Evaluation Scale (FACES-IV)
- Eating Disorder Inventory (EDI)
- Index of Psychological Abuse
- Marital Status Inventory (MSI)
- Michigan Alcohol Screening Test (MAST)
- Multidimensional Measure of Emotional Abuse
- NEO Personality Inventory (NEO-PI)
- NEO Five-Factor Inventory (NEO-FFI)
- Myers-Briggs Type Indicator Personality Inventory (MBTI)
- Partner Abuse Scale—Physical (PASPH)
- Partner Abuse Scale—Non-Physical (PASNP)
- Parenting Alliance Measure (PAM)
- Parenting Relationship Questionnaire (PRQ)
- Parenting Stress Index (PSI)
- Parenting Satisfaction Scale (PSS)
- Partner Relationship Inventory (PRI)
- Physical Abuse of Partner Scale
- PREPARE-ENRICH (Premarital preparation/marital enrichment program)
- Revised Hamilton Rating Scale for Depression (RHRSD)
- Sexual Experiences Survey (SES)
- Revised Conflict Tactics Scales (CTS-2)
- Social Support Questionnaire (SSQ)
- Suicide Probability Scale (SPS)
- Suicidal Ideation Questionnaire (SIQ)
- Trauma Symptom Inventory (TSI)
- Trauma Symptom Checklist for Children (TSCC)
- Women's Experience with Battering (WEB)

The Diagnostic and Statistical Manual of Mental Disorders (DSM)

Any behavior that significantly impairs a client's functioning is considered abnormal, and disorders are diagnosed by traditional standards using the Diagnostic and Statistical Manual of Mental Disorders. At the time of publication of this study guide, the fourth edition (DSM-IV) is the edition that most therapists use. However, American Psychiatric Association released the newly released edition (DSM-V) in May 2013, which is the edition that all therapists are expected to use.

The DSM contains five major axes under which mental disorders are classified:

Axis I	Clinical disorders Other conditions that may be the focus of clinical attention
Axis II	Personality disorders Mental retardation
Axis III	General medical conditions
Axis IV	Psychosocial and environmental problems
Axis V	Global assessment of functioning (code, description of functioning): 91-100 – Person has no problems OR has superior functioning in several areas OR is admired and sought after by others due to positive qualities. No symptoms. 81-90 – Person has few or no symptoms. Good functioning in all areas (social, occupational, or school functioning) with no more than everyday problems or concerns. 71-80 – Person has symptoms/problems that are temporary and expectable reactions to psychosocial stressors. There is no more than slight impairment in areas of psychological functioning (e.g., school, occupational). 61-70 – Mild symptoms in one area OR difficulty in psychological functioning in one of the above-listed areas, but the person is generally functioning well and has a few meaningful interpersonal relationships. 51-60 – Moderate symptoms OR moderate difficulty in one of the above-listed areas. 41-50 – Serious symptoms OR serious impairment in one of the above-listed areas. 31-40 – Some impairment in reality testing OR impairment in speech and communication OR serious impairment in several of these areas: occupational or school functioning, interpersonal relationships, judgment, thinking, or mood.

	21-30 – Presence of hallucinations or delusions that influence behavior OR serious impairment in ability to communicate with others OR serious impairment in judgment OR inability to function in almost all areas (e.g., stays in bed).
	11-20 – There is some danger of harm to self or others OR occasional failure to maintain personal hygiene OR the person is unable to communicate with others (e.g., incoherence, mute).
	1-10 – Persistent danger of harming self or others OR persistent inability to maintain personal hygiene OR serious suicidal attempt.
	0 – Insufficient information.

Source: Based on information from DSM-IV (APA, 2000)

In addition to the five major axes including the individually based Global Assessment of Functioning Scale, which composes axis five, the DSM also provides a Global Assessment of Relational Functioning (GARF) Scale, which may be used to assess the functioning of a family. A summary of this scale follows:

Code	Description
81-100	Relational unit is overall functioning to the satisfaction of its members and observers of the unit.
61-80	Relational unit is functioning, but somewhat unsatisfactory with some complaints resolved over time and some left unresolved.
41-60	Relational unit is dysfunctional with unsatisfying relationships; may still have moments of functioning or providing satisfaction to its members.
21-40	Relational unit is seriously dysfunctional with minimal to no healthy functioning or times of providing satisfaction to its members.
1-20	Relational unit is severely dysfunctional with little to no consistent contact or attachment between its members.
0	Insufficient information.

Source: Based on information from DSM-IV (APA, 2000)

Essential Duties of MFTs

Clinical Recordkeeping

All MFTs are required to maintain proper and accurate clinical records. These may include:

- ❖ Client intake information (e.g., contact information, presenting concerns, medical and psychiatric history, past treatment history)
- ❖ Billing records and receipts
- ❖ Records of therapist-client contact
- ❖ Records of therapist consultation with other professionals on behalf of a client
- ❖ Session progress or process notes
- ❖ Supervision records

Major ethical considerations specific to the maintenance of client records include the following:

- ❖ Principle 3.6 – MFTs are expected to maintain clinical records and ensure their accuracy according to law.

- ❖ Principle 2.4 – MFTs must take steps to protect clients' confidentiality during storage or disposal of client records.

- ❖ Principle 2.5 – MFTs must take steps to protect clients' confidentiality during the movement or closing of a practice or in the event of death.

- ❖ Principle 2.7 – MFTs must take steps to protect clients' confidentiality during the electronic storage of protected information and during clinical communication/billing activities.

In the event that a therapist closes a practice, if a client desires to continue therapy treatment, MFTs are required to provide referral assistance and provide records to the new therapist with the client's consent. Therapists should consult the appropriate laws for how long they are required to retain clients' records after the closing of a case or practice. Generally, this period of time is seven years.

Duty to Report Abuse

All states have laws regarding duties to report child abuse, and some have laws about reporting elder abuse as well. All mental health therapists, as "mandated reporters," are required to report child abuse if they learn of such abuse from victims, perpetrators, or third parties. While therapists must report clear or suspected abuse, they must use clinical judgment and caution to not report unless an incident is considered a reportable offense within their locality so as to not violate client confidentiality. Agencies to which a therapist should report vary by state, and MFTs are encouraged familiarize themselves with their state's child protection and welfare agencies.

Duty to Warn

Therapists are legally obligated to warn others under the following three conditions:

- ❖ The client is determined to likely cause physical harm to himself/herself or others.

- ❖ A therapist's special relationship with with his/her clients and influence over their actions may protect the clients and/or others from being harmed.

- ❖ A client refers to identifiable victims.

This duty came about primarily due to a 1976 Supreme Court ruling, which stemmed from the legal case Tarasoff v. Regents of the University of California. In this case, a client killed a fellow student, and the client's therapist was later sued when it was discovered that threats to kill were disclosed during prior therapy sessions. This is the specific duty to which all mental health therapists are expected to adhere:

> *"When a therapist determines or pursuant to the standards of his profession should determine, that his patient presents a serious danger of violence to another, he incurs an obligation to use reasonable care to protect the intended victim against such danger."*

This duty to warn extends to cases in which therapists discover possible health risks to others from an HIV-positive client only if state law permits and requires such disclosure.

Special Concerns in Marital and Family Therapy

Sexual Involvement with Clients

Inappropriate sexual activity sometimes occurs between therapists and clients, and national studies have demonstrated that as many as eight out of 10 mental health therapists have experienced sexual feelings for at least one client or patient during their careers. There are several serious psychological consequences for clients as a result of therapist-client sexual involvement:

- Cognitive dysfunctions
- Guilt
- Impaired abilities to trust
- Ambivalence
- Isolation and emptiness
- Emotional liability
- Suppressed anger
- Sexual confusion
- Increased suicidality
- Role reversal
- Boundary disturbance

The analysis of Pope and Bouhoutsos (1986) of mental health professionals' sexual involvement with clients identified 10 common scenarios in which therapist-client sexual relationships were most likely to take place:

1. Role trading situations in which the therapist took on the role of the client, and clients took on the role of taking care of the therapist.

2. Sex Therapy scenarios in which therapists convinced patients that sex was a legitimate part of treatment.

3. "As if" scenarios in which patients experienced therapists as all-powerful figures.

4. "Svengali" situations in which therapists used the power of the therapeutic situation to create extreme dependence on their patients' parts.

5. Situations in which drugs were used to induce sexual relationships.

6. Rape scenarios.

7. Situations in which therapists claimed that true love justified breaking professional, ethical, and legal rules.

8. Scenarios in which therapists claimed their actions were accidental or unintentional.

9. "Time out" scenarios in which social relationships developed between sessions and were considered "breaks" from therapy.

10. Situations in which therapists took advantage of patients' desires for non-erotic physical contact.

Therapists should be aware that sexual involvement with clients is *never* acceptable or justifiable. The AAMFT Code of Ethics explicitly states that MFTs are prohibited from sexual contact with clients. Thus, therapists are urged to be aware of the special concerns in this area, abstain from inappropriate behaviors, and accept responsibility for any harmful actions carried out with clients and the resulting consequences.

Technology Use in Family Therapy

Although marriage and family therapy is a relatively young discipline, over its short history, there have been several technologies that have changed the way MFTs conduct their business. There are several forms of technology used by therapists including computers, fax machines, cell phones, and the Internet. Fax machines are often used by MFT's to communicate with insurance and managed care companies regarding client care plans and reimbursement procedures. Fax machines are also often used by MFT's who work with court-ordered clients to communicate with the court system regarding their clients' court-orders and therapy plans. MFTs often use computers to store case notes, keep track of client billing information, store calendars and schedules of client appointments, store client contact information, and communicate with clients via email. MFTs often use cell phones to communicate with clients by call or by text. Also, the Internet is often used in therapy work by both therapists and clients (e.g., to find therapy services).

In recent years, various forms of e-therapy have emerged. Also referred to as "cyber therapy" or online therapy, e-therapy is not an officially recognized form of therapy by the AAMFT. However, some practitioners choose to deliver this form of therapy to clients anyway, regardless of the many ethical challenges it poses. These challenges have been identified by the AAMFT Ethics Committee:

It has not been established that a competent intake and initial assessment can be accomplished without a face-to-face meeting.
The absence of body language and tone of voice certainly diminishes client-therapist communication and makes it harder for the therapist to accurately assess the client's state of mind and nuances of the therapeutic process.
There is a greater risk that the client is not who he/she claims to be, particularly if there is no initial face-to-face meeting.
There are more risks to confidentiality, as electronic transmissions are easily stored, easily forwarded (perhaps unintentionally), may be intercepted, and the entire body of exchanges may be subject to discovery in a legal proceeding – far more data than the usual therapist notes.
It would be more difficult to assist a client with emergencies and appropriate referrals when the client's locale is unfamiliar to the therapist.
It would be more difficult to protect third parties threatened by the client in a locale unfamiliar to the therapist.

Source: Based on information from AAMFT (APA, 2015)

Aside from the ethical issues that are posed by e-therapy, certain legal issues are of concern as well. The AAMFT has identified a couple of these issues:

❖ There is concern that e-therapy could be illegal in some cases because according to U.S. law, family and marriage therapists may practice only in states in which they are licensed as MFTs. Since e-therapy is done over the Internet and could easily involve clients from states outside of those in which their therapists are licensed (perhaps not to the knowledge of the therapist), it may be considered illegal in many instances and can place some MFTs at risk of losing their licenses.

❖ E-therapy involves liability insurance and third-party reimbursements. Since e-therapy is not officially recognized by the AAMFT as a legitimate form of therapy, it is very likely that MFTs who choose to practice this form of therapy will be unable get professional liability coverage from insurance companies (e.g. CPH & Associates). Furthermore, the insurance and managed care companies of clients are unlikely to provide reimbursements for therapy services to MFTs for this form of therapy.

The most prominent concern of using the above-mentioned technologies in family therapy is the ability to maintain confidentiality of clients. According to Principle 2.2 of the AAMFT Code of Ethics: "MFTs must obtain explicit written permission to disclose information that is protected by a client's right to confidentiality." Hence, it is clear that MFTs are ethically obligated to protect their clients' confidentiality. However, many technologies used in family therapy today do pose risks to client confidentiality. For example, when therapists use e-mail to communicate with clients, making an error in just one character in a client's e-mail address could cause a therapist to accidentally send the message to another person. However, even if a therapist verifies his/her client's e-mail address before sending out messages, all information sent via the Internet goes through other channels before reaching the final recipient and may be intercepted and accessed along these channels. If this situation occurs, the confidentiality of a client may be in great jeopardy. As another example, using cell phones and text messages to communicate with a client may put client confidentiality at risk if a therapist's cell phone is lost or stolen or if text messages on shared data plans can be read by family members.

The best practical advice is that no matter how far technology advances and enters the field of family therapy, MFTs must always uphold the ethical and legal guidelines required of their profession. MFTs should exercise common sense and ensure the safety of their clients and themselves. If in doubt over use of technology in family therapy, do not use the technology in question until this doubt has been addressed through professional consultation and a proper review of the ethical and legal principles of the profession.

Chapter 3: Professional Ethics

Professional ethics is an important area for practicing MFTs, and those taking the national MFT exam are expected to know and understand the current code. The following principles are stated from the AAMFT's "Code of Ethics," then summarized:

Principle 1: Responsibility to Clients

"Marriage and family therapists advance the welfare of families and individuals. They respect the rights of those persons seeking their assistance and make reasonable efforts to ensure that their services are used appropriately."

Source: Based on information from AAMFT (APA, 2015)

In general, the responsibilities of MFTs that stem from Principle 1of the ethics code pertain to duties surrounding therapist-client interactions and contact. The 14 sub-principles are summarized below:

1. MFTs must avoid discrimination on any basis in the services they provide to the public.

2. MFTs must obtain informed consent from clients they treat, and the policies and procedures described in consent forms must be understandable to clients. Informed consent must be documented and may be provided only by clients with the mental capacity to consent or clients of appropriate age to consent (see "Example A").

> *Example A*
> *For example, consent for treatment of a minor child must be obtained from a legal guardian or other adult who may legally authorize the treatment of said minor child. In particular, in cases of split custody of a minor child, it is important that MFTs follow their state laws in obtaining appropriate and full consent before providing services to the child.*

3. MFTs must avoid multiple relationships with clients (i.e., relationships with clients outside of the therapist-client relationship), as this may impair clinical judgment or put clients at risk for exploitation.

4. MFTs are banned from engaging in sexual contact with clients or relatives and significant others of clients.

5. MFTs are banned from engaging in sexual contact with former clients or relatives and significant others of clients for two years after treatment termination. It is advised that MFTs never engage in sexual contact with former clients or clients' partners to minimize potential psychological injury. However, if such contact does occur two years after treatment termination, MFTs bear the burden of showing that no harm has occurred to involved and related parties (see "Example B").

> ***Example B***
> *A therapist treats a couple, but after six months, the couple ultimately decides to seek divorce and end therapy. Five years later, he encounters one of the partners in a local coffee shop. After some talking, the former client discloses that she is still single and asks the therapist on a date. In this case, although the two-year mandated period has passed, it is still advised that the therapist decline the date offer to avoid engaging in a sexual relationship with the former client and to minimize the risk of psychological harm should the ex-husband discover the relationship.*

6. MFTs must follow the rules in their state for reporting ethical violations that come to their attention.

7. MFTs avoid using therapeutic relationships to their own benefit.

8. MFTs support the autonomy of their clients by respecting their decisions regarding their relationships and significant others.

9. MFTs may maintain therapeutic relationships if it is deemed that the client is continuing to benefit.

10. MFTs must assist others in securing therapeutic services by providing appropriate referrals in cases where they cannot provide the therapy services themselves.

11. MFTs must not abandon their clients and must ensure that treatment continues, if needed.

12. MFTs must gain and document consent if clients are to be recorded or observed by others in any way (e.g., audio-taped, live observation).

13. In cases where MFTs offer services at a third party's request, they must inform all parties of the expectations for these relationships (e.g., information to remain confidential versus information that is shared, with consent).

14. MFTs must not engage in electronic forms of therapy before first taking steps specific to this form of therapy; mainly, ensuring compliance with state and federal laws and determining the appropriateness of the therapy for a given client.

Principle 2: Confidentiality

Marriage and family therapists have unique confidentiality concerns because the client in a therapeutic relationship may be more than one person. Therapists respect and guard confidences of each individual client.

Source: Based on information from AAMFT (APA, 2015)

This principle of the AAMFT Code of Ethics involves the specific duties that MFTs must take to protect the confidentiality of their clients. The 7 sub-principles are summarized below:

1. MFTs must inform their clients of their rights to confidentiality along with the limits of these rights (e.g., when the disclosure of confidential information is legally necessary).

2. MFTs must obtain explicit written permission to disclose information that is protected by a client's right to confidentiality.

3. MFTs must protect client confidentiality in cases of using client information for non-clinical purposes (e.g., public presentations).

4. MFTs must take steps to protect clients' confidentiality during storage or disposal of client records.

5. MFTs must take steps to protect clients' confidentiality during the movement or closing of a practice or in the event of death.

6. MFTs must take steps to protect clients' identity during consultations with other professionals unless clients have given written consent to disclose their identity. Otherwise, only basic, non-identifying information necessary for consulting purposes may be shared (see "Example C").

> *Example C*
> *An MFT who is receiving clinical case supervision is advised to give her supervisor basic details. Instead of stating, "client is a 43-year-old male who lives in Manhattan, works as a patent attorney, has been married for 3 ½ yrs, and presented with social anxiety disorder" the therapist can further protect her client's identity by stating, "client is a male in his early 40's who lives in New York City, works in the legal field, has been married less than 5 years, and presented with anxiety problems."*

7. MFTs must take steps to protect clients' confidentiality during the electronic storage of protected information and during clinical communication/billing activities.

Principle 3: Professional Competence and Integrity

Marriage and family therapists maintain high standards of professional competence and integrity.

Source: Based on information from AAMFT (APA, 2015)

This principle of the AAMFT Code of Ethics involves the activities that MFTs are expected to take part in or avoid to uphold high standards of professional conduct and remain competent as therapists. The 15 sub-principles are summarized below:

1. MFTs are expected to maintain their professional competency through various means (see "Example D").

> *Example D*
> *It is advised that MFTs take part in continuing education activities, obtain clinical supervision, and/or keep abreast of recent developments in the marital and family therapy field to remain competent in practice.*

2. MFTs are expected to keep abreast of all laws and standards by which they are governed.

3. MFTs are expected to seek assistance when personal issues impair (or present the risk of impairing) their clinical functioning.

4. MFTs are expected to avoid activities that present potential or real conflicts of interest.

5. MFTs, as scholars, are expected to maintain high standards of conduct in all professional activities, both clinical and non-clinical.

6. MFTs are expected to maintain clinical records and ensure their accuracy, according to law.

7. MFTs who develop new skills or practice specialties should use them in clinical activities only after appropriate training and with care to ensure clinical competency.

8. MFTs must avoid all forms of harassment of clients and non-client professionals with whom they have contact (e.g., supervisees).

9. MFTs must avoid exploitation of clients and non-client professionals with whom they have contact.

10. MFTs are expected to avoid giving or receiving gifts from clients that may interfere with the therapist-client relationship or are of high value.

11. MFTs are expected to avoid engaging in clinical activities outside of their scope of training or practice.

12. MFTs are expected to accurately represent the findings of their research and clinical work.

13. MFTs are expected to take special care with any public statements they make regarding their clinical opinions and recommendations.

14. MFTs may not provide both treatment of a minor child and custody evaluations for the same child (see "Example E").

> ***Example E***
> *A therapist treats a couple for marital problems and after several months of sessions, the couple decides to separate and seek divorce. Along with their decision, they agree to have the therapist treat their minor son in order to help him adjust to the transition and deal with the stress of living in a split custody arrangement. A few weeks into the son's treatment, the mother decides to seek full custody and calls the therapist in to testify in court in hopes that the therapist will give an opinion about custody that falls in her favor. In this case, the therapist may cite that doing so would be violating the Code of Ethics and recommend that a custody evaluation be performed by a trained, independent forensic evaluator.*

15. MFTs are considered in violation of the Code of Ethics if they become involved in professional misconduct including involvement in criminal activity, convictions for criminal activity, practicing therapy while impaired, or being non-compliant with ethical violations investigations.

Principle 4: Responsibility to Students, Employees, and Supervisees

Marriage and family therapists do not exploit the trust and dependency of students, employees, and supervisees.

Source: Based on information from AAMFT (APA, 2015)

The fourth principle of the AAMFT Code of Ethics involves the conduct and responsibilities that MFTs have to their students and supervisees. The 7 sub-principles are summarized below:

1. MFTs must avoid exploitation of students and supervisees with whom they have contact.

2. MFTs are not to provide therapy services to their students or supervisees.

3. MFTs are prohibited from having sexual contact with current students or supervisees. If such contact does occur with former students or former supervisees, MFTs bear the burden of showing that no harm has occurred to involved parties.

4. MFTs who oversee students and supervisees do not let them practice or present themselves as competent to practice services beyond their scope.

5. MFTs that oversee students and supervisees help ensure that their services are professional.

6. MFTs must avoid multiple relationships with students and supervisees by declining to accept those with whom they have had a prior personal relationship.

7. MFTs are expected to respect their supervisees' right to confidentiality and not disclose confidences unless written permission has been obtained, it is legally mandated, or information is being shared with other supervisory staff responsible for the supervisee (see "Example F").

> *Example F*
> *A student is supervised by a therapist for several months, and both parties come to develop a very trusting and safe atmosphere for sharing both clinical and personal issues during their meetings. In fact, the student opens up to the supervisor and discloses past struggles with alcohol abuse after a supervision meeting in which they discussed a clinical case with similar abuse issues. Although the disclosure was voluntary and occurred outside of the supervision meeting, in this case, the supervisor is expected to consider the information confidential and not share it with others unless an emergency situation occurs (e.g., the student shows clear signs that he/she has begun abusing alcohol again and puts clients at risk for harm).*

Principle 5: Responsibility to Research Participants

Investigators respect the dignity and protect the welfare of research participants and are aware of applicable laws, regulations, and professional standards governing the conduct of research.

Source: Based on information from AAMFT (APA, 2015)

The fifth principle of the AAMFT Code of Ethics involves the responsibilities that MFTs bear toward protecting research subjects. The 4 sub-principles are summarized below:

1. Research investigators must ensure that their studies are planned with the ethical guidelines of research in mind and in a way that doesn't compromise participants' access to therapeutic services.

2. Research investigators must obtain informed consent from participants and bear in mind that the ability to give consent may be affected if the participant is receiving clinical services (see "Example G").

> *Example G*
> *Often times, clients who receive therapy services from community agencies do so because such services tend to be provided at low or no cost. Therefore, when research studies may be conducted at such agencies, it is advised that measures be taken to ensure proper study design (e.g., obtaining voluntary, informed consent from all participating clients), but also that special care be given to ensure that clients are offered comparable treatment options outside of the research study that are as readily accessible and affordable as those offered through the research study.*

3. Research investigators inform participants of their right to withdraw from research or decline participation, and they make efforts to avoid multiple relationships with participants.

4. Research data is to be protected by participants' right to confidentiality, and research participants are informed when there is a possibility that their data may be obtained by others such as family members.

Principle 6: Responsibility to the Profession

Marriage and family therapists respect the rights and responsibilities of professional colleagues and participate in activities that advance the goals of the profession.

Source: Based on information from AAMFT (APA, 2015)

The sixth principle of the AAMFT Code of Ethics involves the responsibilities that MFTs bear toward advancing and protecting the marital and family therapy profession. The 8 sub-principles are summarized below:

1. In cases where MFTs are employees or members of other organizations, MFTs must continue to uphold the AAMFT Code of Ethics and act accordingly. Actions required for other organizations that conflict with this duty are expected to be resolved in a way that does not fully or partially compromise this standard (See "Example H").

> ***Example H***
> *A therapist accepts a position as a member of a newly formed community panel with the purpose of assisting families who own family businesses and experience problems with family functioning, financial planning, and business decisions. The panel is composed of various professionals including MFTs, financial planners, and attorneys. The panel's leader designs a referrals program for the panel members in which each member agrees to send one another referrals in exchange for a small "kick back" (financial compensation) for each referral. In this case, the therapist would not be violating the Code of Ethics by remaining a panel member, but would be doing so by agreeing to participate in the referrals program. Thus, it is advised that the therapist decline to participate.*

2. MFTs must give credit to contributing authors of publications.

3. MFTs must not accept credit for publications or research work produced by their students unless appropriate (e.g., providing a substantial contribution that would normally require credit according to standard publication practice).

4. MFTs must not plagiarize the work of other authors or researchers.

5. MFTs work to ensure the accuracy of their publications.

6. MFTs advance the needs of their communities and society at-large by participating in pro bono professional activities.

7. MFTs help to advocate for legislation that further promotes the profession and best serves the needs of their communities and society at-large.

8. MFTs welcome and encourage public participation in advancing and regulating the practice of their profession.

Principle 7: Financial Arrangements

Marriage and family therapists make financial arrangements with clients, third party payers, and supervisees that are reasonable and conform to accepted professional practices.

Source: Based on information from AAMFT (APA, 2015)

The seventh principle of the AAMFT Code of Ethics involves the responsibilities that MFTs bear regarding financial practices within their profession. The 6 sub-principles are summarized below:

1. MFTs maintain financial integrity by declining financial incentives for providing referrals.

2. MFTs disclose their policies surrounding client payments (e.g., acceptable payment methods, fee charges for cancellations) before providing therapeutic services.

3. MFTs provide to their clients "reasonable notice" before collection actions are taken for unpaid balances. If such actions are taken, the therapist continues to respect clients' right to confidentiality.

4. MFTs truthfully represent their services rendered to clients, supervisees, and third parties (e.g., insurance companies).

5. MFTs generally abstain from bartering practices for therapy services and take protective measures when engaging in such practices (e.g., written contract).

6. MFTs may not withhold records from clients due to non-payment for services rendered.

Principle 8: Advertising

Marriage and family therapists engage in appropriate informational activities including those that enable the public, referral sources, or others to choose professional services on an informed basis.

Source: Based on information from AAMFT (APA, 2015)

The eighth principle of the AAMFT Code of Ethics involves the responsibilities that MFTs bear regarding advertising practices within their profession. The 8 sub-principles are summarized below:

1. MFTs accurately represent themselves as therapists including their scope of practice, education/training, and experience.

2. MFTs provide necessary information in all forms of advertising materials about their services to enable the public to make informed treatment choices.

3. MFTs accurately and truthfully represent their professional affiliations (e.g., membership in professional organizations; see "Example I").

> *Example I*
> *Therapists may become members of several professional organizations and associations over the course of their careers and, in some cases, may let such memberships lapse (e.g., unintentionally due to missing dues deadlines). If a particular membership does lapse, it would be considered unethical for a therapist to continue to represent himself/herself to the public as a member of a particular organization on one's business cards or professional website, for example.*

4. MFTs accurately and truthfully represent their professional identities on all forms of professional identification (e.g., business cards, office letterhead).

5. MFTs provide references to accredited/approved educational institutions only when listing their qualifying and relevant credentials.

6. MFTs correct inaccurate information regarding their credentials and services.

7. MFTs provide accurate information about the qualifications of employees and supervisees.

8. MFTs do not represent specialty services unless qualified to do so by training and experience.

Test Your Knowledge

1. Which of the following theories could classify someone as "avoidant fearful" in his/her interactions with others?
    A. Attachment
    B. Communication
    C. Object relations
    D. All of the above

2. A schema is a major concept within which model of family therapy?
    A. Solution-Focused
    B. Structural
    C. Strategic
    D. Cognitive Behavioral

3. One's ability to distinguish and separate his/her own emotional and intellectual functioning from that of others is referred to as:
    A. Emotional cutoff
    B. Differentiation of self
    C. Emotional maturity
    D. Extraction

4. Calling one's self a "loser" or a "big failure" would be an example of which type of cognitive error within Cognitive Behavioral Therapy?
    A. Personalization
    B. Mislabeling
    C. Mimicking
    D. Jumping to conclusions

5. A central tenet of Contextual Therapy regarding family interactions is that:
    A. Emotion organizes attachment behaviors and the way the self and others are experienced.
    B. Family members strive to promote fairness by unconsciously forming ties and loyalties with other members.
    C. Families that are not in touch with the present are "emotionally dead."
    D. None of the above

6. Within Emotionally Focused Therapy, withdrawers are those partners who tend to turn away from their partners (e.g., by avoiding or leaving arguments) and turn down the "emotional heat" in the relationship in order to protect and preserve it. Which primary feelings do such partners often experience in relation to their partners?
   A. Rejected
   B. Afraid of failure
   C. Inadequate
   D. All of the above

7. Placating, blaming, computing, and distracting are all examples of what within Experiential Therapy:
   A. Examples of how clients avoid completing homework assignments
   B. Poses used by people to hide their true feelings
   C. The factors that determine whether a family will improve in its functioning
   D. Behaviors that may lead to disorder in children if parents display them often

8. Michael White and David Epston are both founders/leaders of which model of family therapy?
   A. Solution-Focused Therapy
   B. Psychoanalytic Family Therapy
   C. Cognitive Behavioral Therapy
   D. Narrative Therapy

9. Within Emotionally Focused Therapy, second order changes are those that:
   A. Constitute a change in the structure of the relationship
   B. Are ordered as a part of the second homework assignment
   C. Are considered secondary to helping clients reach their main goals
   D. None of the above

10. A couple and their two adult sons present to therapy and report that they've recently attempted to reconnect after years of conflict and long periods of not speaking to one another, following the divorce of the parents and the subsequent drug abuse issues of the youngest son. What would be considered the most appropriate score for them on the Global Assessment of Relational Functioning (GARF) Scale?
    A. 90
    B. 50
    C. 25
    D. 0

11. What should a therapist do if a client refuses to pay his/her bill for services rendered and requests his/her records be transferred to a new therapist to continue treatment?
    A. Tell the client that his/her records will be released promptly after the outstanding balance is paid
    B. Ask the client for the contact information of his/her new therapist, then contact the new therapist and let him/her know that the records are being held until the client pays his/her bill
    C. Tell the client his/her records will be released to the new therapist, and take steps to give the client advanced notice of bill collection efforts
    D. All of the above

12. A family enters therapy because the children do not respect the rules set forth by the parents and constantly get into trouble at school. Which model of family therapy would most likely be recommended for this family?
    A. Psychoanalytic
    B. Experiential
    C. Bowen Family Systems
    D. Structural

13. Which of the following concepts refers to the unhealthy pattern that develops when two people avoid conflict by bringing in a third person or entity?
    A. Triangulation
    B. Separation
    C. Enmeshment
    D. Fusion

14. Which principle from the AAMFT Code of Ethics requires that MFTs not participate in the activities of other organizations that conflict with a therapist's ability to follow the Code of Ethics?
    A. Responsibility to Clients
    B. Responsibility to the Profession
    C. Professional Competence and Integrity
    D. Both A and C

15. According to the AAMFT Code of Ethics, why are MFTs expected to avoid giving or receiving gifts from a client?
    A. Because it may require that the therapist give the client a gift in return that is of equal or greater value, which may financially strain the therapist
    B. Because it may interfere with the therapist-client relationship
    C. Because gifts may contain hidden meanings about the client's psychological well-being that the therapist may or may not be able to decipher
    D. All of the above

16. Family members who find themselves "enmeshed" with one another are said to have which kind of boundaries?
    A. Clear
    B. Rigid
    C. Diffuse
    D. All of the above

17. Which of the following statements about an MFT's relationships with former clients is true?
    A. A therapist may engage in sexual contact with a former client at any time.
    B. A therapist must wait two years after the termination of treatment before engaging in sexual contact with a former client.
    C. A therapist must wait five years after the termination of treatment before engaging in sexual contact with a former client.
    D. A therapist should never engage in sexual contact with a former client.

18. A therapist treats a couple, and after 6 months, the couple ultimately decides to end therapy and get divorced. Years later, the therapist encounters one of the partners in a local coffee shop. After some talking, the former client discloses that she is single and asks the therapist on a date. The mandated period of time has passed that allows therapist to be intimately involved with the client. In this case, it is advised that:
    A. The therapist decline the date offer and offer the client the opportunity to resume treatment
    B. The therapist accept the date offer, but tell the former client that the relationship must immediately be reported to the state ethics board
    C. The therapist decline the date offer to avoid having a sexual relationship with the former client and to minimize the risk of psychological harm should the ex-husband discover the relationship
    D. All of the above

19. Online therapy presents a challenge to the practice of therapy because:
    A. Of the greater risk that the client is not who he/she claims to be
    B. The lack of vocal tone and body language weakens client-therapist communication
    C. The increased difficulty of protecting third parties threatened by the client
    D. All of the above

20. Personality disorders fall on which axis in the DSM?
    A. I
    B. II
    C. III
    D. IV

21. According to attachment theory, a major benefit of healthy relationships is that they:
    A. Provide a buffer against the effects of stress and are an optimal development environment
    B. Help family members maintain positive attitudes toward one another
    C. Help people distinguish and separate their own emotional and intellectual functioning from that of others
    D. Help individuals and families resist the negative influences within larger society

22. Which concept refers to the expected rights of children within families inherent to being born?
    A. Filial loyalty
    B. Consolidation
    C. Transgenerational entitlement
    D. Symbolic drawing of life space

23. Which model of family therapy is closely related to Experiential Therapy?
    A. EFT
    B. Psychoanalytic
    C. Cognitive Behavioral
    D. Strategic

24. Which model of family therapy places the most emphasis on changing client language use to promote change?
    A. Solution-Focused
    B. Structural
    C. Bowen Family Systems
    D. MRI

25. Which model of family therapy employs the use of genograms to help clients reach their goals?
    A. Solution-Focused
    B. Bowen Family Systems
    C. Strategic
    D. Structural

26. Which of the following is an aspect of family therapy practice dealt with in the legal case Tarasoff v. Regents of the University of California?
    A. Duty to warn
    B. Duty to report abuse
    C. Duty to maintain accurate clinical records
    D. Duty to protect confidentiality

27. Which of the following is NOT a principle of the AAMFT Code of Ethics?
    A. Responsibility to Research Participants
    B. Advertising
    C. Confidentiality
    D. Responsibility to Maintain Privacy

28. True or False: It would be considered unethical for a therapist to continue to post his/her membership in a professional organization on his/her website if the organization is NOT approved by the AAMFT as an "affiliated" organization.
    A. True
    B. False

29. True or False: The AAMFT Code of Ethics states that MFTs should correct inaccurate information regarding their credentials and services.
    A. True
    B. False

30. Which of the following concepts involves viewing and restating a client's problems or behaviors in alternative, more positive ways?
    A. Reframing
    B. Rejoining
    C. Scaling
    D. Clarifying

31. Which of the following theorists helped found Solution-Focused Therapy?
    A. Jay Haley
    B. Salvador Minuchin
    C. Peggy Papp
    D. Steve de Shazer

32. Which model of family therapy includes the concept of "good-enough parenting?"
    A. Experiential
    B. Object Relations
    C. Contextual
    D. Structural

33. Which of the following therapy techniques could most help a client struggling with an eating disorder avoid defining his/her personal identity by the disorder (e.g., "I'm a bulimic")?
    A. Externalizing
    B. Letter-writing
    C. Desensitization
    D. Behavior modification

34. Which of the following is NOT a "pose" that people use to hide their true feelings, according to Experiential Therapy?
    A. Placater
    B. Blamer
    C. Withdrawer
    D. Computer

35. Which of the following is a key skill used by family therapists?
    A. Mirroring
    B. Strengthening
    C. Splitting
    D. Empathic listening

36. Which type of team is used in Narrative Therapy and consists of several therapists who observe family sessions and share their reactions with the family following a session?
    A. Reflecting
    B. Exploratory
    C. Family sculpting
    D. Validation

37. Which principle from the AAMFT Code of Ethics requires that MFTs represent themselves accurately including their scope of practice, education/training, and experience?
    A. Professional Competence and Integrity
    B. Advertising
    C. Responsibility to Clients
    D. Responsibility to the Profession

38. Asking a client a question like "Give me a number between 1 and 10, with 1 being the worst and 10 being the best, to describe how bad you think your communication is with your partner at this time?" would be an example of which therapy technique?
    A. Joining
    B. Clarifying narrow binds
    C. Scaling
    D. Miracle question

39. A couple presents to therapy, and the husband explains that every time they try to have sex, he wonders whether or not he's pleasuring his wife and loses his erection. Which technique should a therapist use to help him overcome this problem?
    A. Cognitive restructuring
    B. Restraining
    C. Positioning
    D. Sensate focus

40. Which of the following therapy techniques is designed to make it more difficult for a client to maintain a symptom than to give it up?
    A. Ordeal
    B. Directive
    C. Consolidation
    D. Desensitization

41. A key technique in Attachment Therapy is identifying attachment styles. Which of the following is an attachment style within Attachment Therapy?
    A. Secure
    B. Anxious
    C. Avoidant fearful and dismissing
    D. All of the above

42. Which of the following is an attachment style within Attachment Therapy?
    A. Secure
    B. Anxious
    C. Avoidant Fearful and Dismissing
    D. All of the above

43. Which of the following is NOT a common attachment need within Attachment Therapy?
    A. Need to be and feel loved
    B. Need to be accepted
    C. Need to be comforted
    D. Need for attention

44. Which of the following aspects of couples therapy does Attachment Therapy focus on?
    A. Attachment needs of partners and engagement or disengagement forms and addressing "attachment injuries" or disruptions
    B. Using emotion as the agent of therapeutic change
    C. Creating a "safe space" for partners to be authentic within therapy sessions and shaping new bonding responses between partners
    D. All of the above

45. True or False: The goal of couples therapy based on Attachment Therapy is to address attachment concerns, reduce attachment insecurities, and create a secure bond between partners.
    A. True
    B. False

46. Which of the following is a basic assumption of Cognitive Behavioral Therapy?
    A. Behavior is maintained by its consequences.
    B. There is an intrinsic, unbreakable connection between cognitions, emotions, and behaviors.
    C. People's interpretation of the behavior of others affects the way they respond.
    D. All of the above

47. Which of the following is NOT a key concept in Cognitive Behavioral Therapy?
    A. Transference
    B. Affect
    C. Behaviors
    D. Cognitions

48. _____ is one's display of emotion.
    A. Affect
    B. Behavior
    C. Cognition
    D. Cognitive distortion

49. _____ are the actions that one takes.
    A. Affects
    B. Behaviors
    C. Cognitions
    D. Cognitive distortions

50. _____ are one's thought processes.
    A. Affects
    B. Behaviors
    C. Cognitions
    D. Cognitive distortions

51. _____ are errors in one's thought processes.
    A. Affects
    B. Behaviors
    C. Cognitions
    D. Cognitive distortions

52. _____ is a cognitive distortion wherein an individual views things in black and white, rigid categories (e.g., "My imperfect score means I'm a failure").
    A. Disqualifying the positive
    B. Mental filter
    C. Overgeneralization
    D. All or nothing thinking

53. _____ is a cognitive distortion wherein an individual views one negative occurrence as a continuous, persistent pattern of defeat.
    A. Jumping to conclusions
    B. Disqualifying the positive
    C. Mental filter
    D. Overgeneralization

54. _____ is a cognitive distortion wherein an individual fixates on one negative detail and dwells on it disregarding any of the positive details.
    A. Disqualifying the positive
    B. Mental filter
    C. Overgeneralization
    D. All or nothing thinking

55. _____ is a cognitive distortion wherein an individual insists that positive experiences don't count and rejects them; this helps maintain a negative belief system that may actually be contradicted by everyday experiences.
    A. Jumping to conclusions
    B. Disqualifying the positive
    C. Overgeneralization
    D. All or nothing thinking

56. _____ is a cognitive distortion wherein an individual interprets an occurrence as negative despite definitive facts supporting a positive conclusion.
    A. Jumping to conclusions
    B. Disqualifying the positive
    C. Mental filter
    D. Overgeneralization

57. Which of the following is a relationship dimension on which Contextual Therapy is centered?
    A. The facts of people's lives, like localities, health conditions, and marital status
    B. Psychology, which is described as the cognitive and emotional attributes that individuals assign to facts in their lives
    C. Transactions or family relationship patterns
    D. All of the above

58. Which of the following is NOT a key concept in Emotionally Focused Therapy?
    A. Attachment
    B. Consolidation
    C. Pursuers
    D. Transference

59. Which of the following is a key technique in Emotionally Focused Therapy?
    A. Alliance-building
    B. Blamer-softening
    C. Cycle de-escalation
    D. All of the above

60. _____ is a key technique in Emotionally Focused Therapy in which the aim is to create an alliance where both partners feel safe and accepted by the therapist and begin to have confidence that the therapist understands their goals/needs and will be able to help them.
    A. Alliance-building
    B. Blamer-softening
    C. Emphatic interpretation
    D. Empathic reflection

61. _____ is a key technique in Emotionally Focused Therapy that occurs when the previously more active and hostile spouse takes a risk by expressing his/her own vulnerabilities and attachment needs, which allows interactions to challenge the relationship's level of trust.
    A. Alliance-building
    B. Blamer-softening
    C. Emphatic interpretation
    D. Empathic reflection

62. _____ is a key technique in Emotionally Focused Therapy that urges one of the partners to expand on his/her present experience, inferring from the therapist's relational context or experience of the person, in order to process his/her experience one step further.
    A. Alliance-building
    B. Blamer-softening
    C. Emphatic interpretation
    D. Empathic reflection

63. _____ is a key technique in Emotionally Focused Therapy that involves the therapist giving reflections of each partner's experience of the relationship and of sequences of interaction, both positive and negative, that characterize the interaction.
    A. Alliance-building
    B. Blamer-softening
    C. Emphatic interpretations
    D. Empathic reflection

64. _____ is a key technique in Emotionally Focused Therapy where the therapist follows the client's experience and focuses on the partial, tentative, or "in process" edges of the experience. They invite the client to process a particular experience further, letting new aspects be revealed, reorganizing the experience.
    A. Alliance-building
    B. Blamer-softening
    C. Emphatic interpretations
    D. Evocative responding

65. Which of the following is NOT an underlying assumption about human nature in Experiential Therapy?
    A. People want to increase their abilities to be sensitive and genuine with each other, although the strategies they use sometimes to achieve these goals are flawed.
    B. Low-self esteem blocks people's ability to share their emotional experiences, resulting in dysfunctional family relationships.
    C. Families that are not in touch with the present are "emotionally dead."
    D. People want to be isolated from society.

66. _____ involves pacifying others, glossing over differences, and acting defensive of others when conflict arises.
   A. Placating
   B. Blaming
   C. Computing
   D. Distracting
   E. Leveling

67. _____ involves being judgmental of others and comparing and/or complaining when conflict arises.
   A. Placating
   B. Blaming
   C. Computing
   D. Distracting
   E. Leveling

68. _____ involves using logic, lecturing, and outside authority when conflict arises.
   A. Placating
   B. Blaming
   C. Computing
   D. Distracting
   E. Leveling

69. _____ involves changing the subject, feigning misunderstanding, being quiet, and pretending to be weak and helpless when conflict arises.
   A. Placating
   B. Blaming
   C. Computing
   D. Distracting
   E. Leveling

70. _____ involves displaying affect and behavior consistent and appropriate to a given situation.
   A. Placating
   B. Blaming
   C. Computing
   D. Leveling

71. Which of the following is a key concept in Narrative Therapy?
    A. Deconstruction
    B. Dominant story
    C. Problem-saturated stories
    D. All of the above

72. Which of the following is NOT a technique in Narrative Therapy?
    A. Externalizing problems
    B. Exploring unique outcomes
    C. Letter-writing
    D. Reframing

73. Which of the following is an assumption underlying Object Relations Therapy?
    A. The basic human motive is the search for satisfying relationships with other humans.
    B. Unconscious forces from childhood determine the behavioral patterns that develop in adulthood and in adult relationships.
    C. Intrapsychic pathology commonly appears as relationship distress.
    D. All of the above

74. Which of the following is NOT a key concept of Object Relations Therapy?
    A. False self
    B. Ordeals
    C. Good-enough parenting
    D. Idealization

75. Which of the following is a main technique in Object Relations Therapy?
    A. Empathic listening
    B. Interpretation
    C. Transference
    D. All of the above

76. _____ is a key technique in Object Relations Therapy that concerts attention to detect latent meaning behind speech or interactions.
    A. Empathic listening
    B. Interpretation
    C. Transference
    D. Countertransference

77. _____ is a key technique in Object Relations Therapy in which the therapist offers the client a subjective meaning or motive behind a reported or observed behavior, affect, or opinion.
    A. Empathic listening
    B. Interpretation
    C. Transference
    D. Countertransference

78. _____ is a key technique in Object Relations Therapy in which a client's feelings, drives, attitudes, and fantasies are being unconsciously shifted onto the therapist; these aspects are displaced from unresolved responses to people who were significant to the client in the past.
    A. Empathic listening
    B. Interpretation
    C. Transference
    D. Countertransference

79. _____ is a key technique in Object Relations Therapy that analyzes spontaneous reactions toward a client's transference. Considered a vital source of information about intrapsychic deficits, this involves the therapist's unconscious emotional responses to a client that are reminiscent of feelings he/she experienced with a person in the past.
    A. Empathic listening
    B. Interpretation
    C. Transference
    D. Countertransference

80. Which of the following is an assumption in Psychoanalytic Family Therapy?
    A. Neuroses stem from childhood conflicts that were generated by colliding forces of inner drives and external experiences.
    B. Our innate drives form the basis for understanding a person's motivation, conflicts, and symptomatic behavior.
    C. Family relationships impact an individual's character formation (i.e. symptomatic behavior).
    D. All of the above

Test Your Knowledge—Answers

1. A.
2. D.
3. B.
4. B.
5. A.
6. D.
7. B.
8. D.
9. A.
10. C.
11. C.
12. D.
13. A.
14. B.
15. B.
16. C.
17. D.
18. C.
19. D.
20. B.
21. A.
22. C.
23. A.
24. A.
25. B.
26. A.
27. D.
28. B.
29. A.
30. A.
31. D.
32. B.
33. A.
34. C.
35. D.
36. A.
37. B.
38. C.
39. D.
40. A.
41. D.
42. D.
43. D.
44. D.
45. A.
46. D.
47. A.
48. A.
49. B.
50. C.
51. D.
52. D.
53. D.
54. B.
55. B.
56. A.
57. D.
58. D.
59. D.
60. A.
61. B.
62. C.
63. D.
64. D.
65. D.
66. A.
67. B.
68. C.
69. D.
70. D.
71. D.
72. D.
73. D.
74. B.
75. D.
76. A.
77. B.
78. C.
79. D.
80. D.

Additional Study Resources

Association of Marital and Family Therapy Regulatory Board (AMFTRB)

The AMFTRB is the regulatory association of Marital and Family Therapists in the United States. Those preparing to take the national MFT exam may find it helpful to review the following additional resources from AMFTRB:

- For MFT exam specifications including specific information on exam construction, please refer to the AMFTRB's "Exam Information" web page: www.amftrb.org/exam.cfm.

- For answers to frequently asked questions about the MFT examination, please refer to AMFTRB's "FAQ" web page: www.amftrb.org/faq.cfm.

- For links to the MFT State Licensing Boards within the United States, please refer to AMFTRB's "Board Listing" web page: www.amftrb.org/stateboards.cfm.

Contact Information	
Website: www.amftrb.org Email: info@amftrb.org Phone: 719-388-1615	Mailing Address: Lois Paff Bergen, PhD AMFTRB Executive Director 1843 Austin Bluffs Parkway Colorado Springs, CO 80918

American Association for Marriage and Family Therapy (AAMFT)

The AAMFT is the professional association for the marriage and family therapy field in the United States and Canada. It is composed of individual state and provincial divisions. Those preparing to take the national MFT exam may wish to consider joining the AAMFT and their local state division for additional professional support and networking.

Contact Information	
Website: www.aamft.org Email: central@aamft.org Phone: 703-838-9808	Mailing Address: 112 South Alfred Street Alexandria, VA 22314

FREE DVD **FREE DVD**

Miller Analogies Test (MAT) DVD from Trivium Test Prep!

Dear Customer,

Thank you for purchasing from Trivium Test Prep! We're honored to help you prepare for your exam.

To show our appreciation, we're offering a **FREE** *MFT Essential Test Tips* **DVD by Trivium Test Prep**. Our DVD includes 35 test preparation strategies that will make you successful on your exam. All we ask is that you email us your feedback and describe your experience with our product. Amazing, awful, or just so-so: we want to hear what you have to say!

To receive your **FREE** *MFT Essential Test Tips* DVD, please email us at 5star@triviumtestprep.com. Include "Free 5 Star" in the subject line and the following information in your email:

1. The title of the product you purchased.
2. Your rating from 1 – 5 (with 5 being the best).
3. Your feedback about the product, including how our materials helped you meet your goals and ways in which we can improve our products.
4. Your full name and shipping address so we can send your **FREE** *MFT Essential Test Tips* DVD.

If you have any questions or concerns please feel free to contact us directly at 5star@triviumtestprep.com. Thank you!

- Trivium Test Prep Team

www.ingramcontent.com/pod-product-compliance
Lightning Source LLC
Chambersburg PA
CBHW081423230426
43668CB00016B/2328